ry Sources

Living Proof: A Local History Activity Pack

Additional materials are also available for use in teaching local history study units of the National Curriculum at Key Stage 2. *Living Proof: A Local History Activity Pack* contains a wealth of historical evidence and practical teaching tools, including photocopiable material and teacher notes.

Written by the authors of this book, the pack has been co-produced by Hodder & Stoughton and Channel 4 Schools. It can be ordered from the following addresses:

Hodder & Stoughton Educational
Bookpoint Ltd
FREEPOST OF 1488
Abingdon
Oxon
OX14 4YY

quote ISBN 0 340 68374 0

Channel 4 Schools
PO Box 100
Warwick
CV34 6TZ

quote IPC 156571

Using Local History Sources

A teachers' guide for the National Curriculum

James Griffin
David Eddershaw

with contributions by
Carol Anderson and Greg Stragnell

Hodder & Stoughton

A MEMBER OF THE HODDER HEADLINE GROUP

British Library Cataloguing in Publication Data

A Catalogue for this title is available from the British Library

First published in Great Britain 1994
Revised edition published in Great Britain 1996

© 1996 James Griffin and David Eddershaw

Impression number 10 9 8 7 6 5 4 3 2 1
Year   1998 1997 1996

ISBN 0–340–68805–X

Produced by GreenGate Publishing Services, Tonbridge, Kent
Printed and bound in Great Britain for Hodder and Stoughton Educational, a
division of Hodder Headline plc, 338 Euston Road, London NW1 3BH, by
Bath Press, Bath

Contents

Acknowledgements

In particular, we wish to thank Carol Anderson and Greg Stragnell, experts in the fields of artefacts and the application of IT to local history, for their important contributions to this book.

There are also a number of other people to whom we owe a great deal. We are indebted to the staffs of many reference and local studies libraries around the country, especially The Centre for Oxfordshire Studies; Oxfordshire Archives; and Oxfordshire County Museum – all part of Oxfordshire County Council's Department of Leisure and Arts. We also thank Nottinghamshire County Records Office for making an inventory and a school logbook available; and Hull Local Studies Library (Humberside County Libraries) for help selecting and reproducing maps. The staff of the Ordnance Survey Information Service gave invaluable advice on parts of the text of Chapter 7, for which we are most grateful.

Our thanks also go to the following people. To Paul Churchouse for suggesting the idea in the first place; to David Kennedy, who helped with Chapter 3, and to whom we are also indebted for producing fine drawings of buildings from our vague ideas; to Bob Baldwin for suggestions and helpful reading matter also relating to Chapter 3; and to David Lea for help and support throughout the whole project.

We acknowledge several sources for the use of illustrations:

Oxfordshire Museums for figures in Chapter 2.

Figures 4.1 and 4.2 are reproduced with the permission of Her Majesty's Stationery Office.

Figure 7.4 is reproduced with permission from the 1892 Ordnance Survey map.

Figure 7.6 is reproduced with permission from the Cambridge University Collection of Air Photographs.

The illustrations in Chapter 8, and the cover photographs, are reproduced by permission of Birmingham Library Services.

Figures 10.1 and 10.2 are reproduced with permission from Cheshire County Council Archives and Local Studies

For Figures 11.1 and 11.2 we are indebted to the Oxfordshire Photographic Archive (Centre for Oxfordshire Studies).

Our thanks too to Anne Thorn and Stuart Hargreaves for teachers' eye views; and finally, to our families for putting up with hours of being antisocial in commune with our keyboards!

Preface to the Revised edition

This new edition coincides with the production of an innovative series of Channel 4 television programmes for Key Stage 2, *Living Proof*. The programmes take four main evidence types (Buildings, Documents, Pictures and Artefacts) and explore their use within the context of the five prescribed study periods for Key Stage 2. All this is done in the format of an interactive quiz show, where the children watching are presented with a rapid series of questions to answer.

We are delighted that Hodder and Stoughton and Channel 4 have endorsed this new edition and recommended it to teachers in addition to their other supplementary material for *Living Proof*.

The revisions we have made for this new edition bring the book into line with the 1995 changes to the history National Curriculum. The requirement to teach a Local History Unit at Key Stage 2 remains, as does the need to investigate a variety of sources at both Key Stages 2 and 3.

JG and DE
May 1996

1 Introduction

This book is intended to increase teachers' awareness of some widely available local sources, and their confidence in using them. It is not just about teaching local history, but also about using these local sources to support the wider themes of British history.

It is aimed at Key Stages 1, 2 and 3. The specifically local history study units occur here and will often be taught by those who are not specialist historians, and who may not have any previous experience of using primary source material. It is intended mainly to help them, but we hope it will also be useful to many other teachers who wish to make the most of the National Curriculum requirement that children should be presented with a variety of sources at all Key Stages. As the matrix on page 7 shows, the local sources in this book can contribute to very many of the Study Units at Key Stages 1, 2 and 3.

Each chapter has a section which points out the relevance of the source to particular Units, but it is just as important to see them in relation to the Key Elements. Indeed, local history offers some of the best opportunities for developing real historical skills simply because it encourages the use of primary sources. Such material inevitably requires a range of skills to understand, extract and interpret information, and to evaluate the reliability of the sources themselves, activities which are an essential part of Key Element 4, Historical Enquiry.

The documentary sources described here should be available in most parts of the country, and will usually be found in main libraries with local studies collections, county or city record offices or special local studies centres, where these exist. Don't be afraid to ask; you will find archivists and librarians very willing to help. It is always a good idea, however, to ring up or write first and explain what you are looking for (and ask if there is an education officer). Don't just turn up and expect them to be able to give the time to searching out suitable examples immediately.

There are basically two ways in which local sources can be used. They can provide local examples to illustrate the themes of national history (sometimes perhaps providing evidence which conflicts with common generalisations), or they can be at the centre of a local study.

A school building with *British Schools, 1856* carved on the front clearly illustrates the point that elementary education was provided by Voluntary Societies in the nineteenth century. Because children are able to see a local example here in their own town, their learning is reinforced, and Victorian Britain becomes a little more real and relevant to them.

The second approach might involve the study of family life in their town in Victorian times, and could lead them to use the census returns to check the accuracy of the statement that 'Victorians had large families'. They would need to consider what 'large' means in this context, and then to see if the local evidence supports the statement. That leads on to such questions as 'Were all the families large?', 'Was there a difference between rich and poor?', and so on. Children should also go on to consider the validity of the sample they are using. Questions like these promote real historical thinking, but they are not beyond the reach of Key Stage 2 and 3 pupils.

Local history was being taught in good primary and secondary schools before the advent of the National Curriculum. The difference is in the type of structured approach now required.

The Local History unit must relate to a significant historical issue. It is no longer enough for pupils to study the history of, say, Penzance from the Conquest to the present day for its own sake. Now they must concentrate on a particular topic, such as 'Education in Penzance', or 'How did people earn a living in Penzance in Victorian times?', or 'Penzance during the Second World War'. Instead of local history being so wide ranging (and sometimes aimless), it is now purposefully focused, and set within clearly defined boundaries.

At the same time, one of the basic problems in delivering National Curriculum history at Key Stage 1 and 2, is that most primary school teachers are under pressure: they are required to be experts in every field. Teachers with specialist knowledge in music, for example, must be able to teach history to the same standards as those with history training. The natural response of many may therefore be to rush out and buy all the ready-made 'off-the-peg' kits for teaching each of the Units. But good local history teaching is about more than simply getting your pack of local materials from the nearest library or record office. This book aims to deal in a practical way with good ideas for using such material in the classroom, appropriate to the Key Elements of the National Curriculum.

Whether or not you have a history background, there are many different kinds of local material available to you. So, which should you use, and how can this book help?

Principally, we can assure teachers that helpful local material is available. What is more, children are more likely to learn from local sources just because it is familiar to them.

Layout

Our layout is as follows.

BACKGROUND

We begin each chapter with a descriptive section, including what the source can tell us, bearing the highlighted symbol which heads this paragraph. We do not go to great lengths: there are many good, accessible books which can do this much better than we can.

WHERE?

Next, we show where this material can be found. Note, though, that there is no substitute for personal research into the sources you choose; our guide is only an introduction. If you are lucky enough to have a local advisory and resource centre you may be able to get further help there.

HSUs

We then indicate how the material will tie in with the History Study Units of the National Curriculum.

ACTIVITIES

Fourthly, we give examples of what can be done in the classroom with this material. We do our best to indicate in these, which part of the History NC will be benefited by each activity.

IT

The application of information technology to the source concerned follows, though not every chapter has such a section.

PROBLEMS

Finally, we cover particular difficulties the children may meet in using each source. Overcoming these may well provide just the challenging stimulus needed to bring history alive to the class.

Chapters may also be divided into other relevant sections; but all are highlighted in the way we have indicated above.

Cross curricula links

It is important to make links between the programmes of study for history and other subjects in the curriculum, and there are opportunities for doing this when using local documents and sources. It is probably fairly common practice to co-ordinate the history local study unit at KS2 with the local area study which forms part of the geography curriculum. Specific skills also overlap between subject areas, and Key Elements in other subjects can be met when working with the local history source materials included in this book.

Artefacts are subject to changing designs, and this is an important consideration of technology, which also covers the materials used. The study of local buildings creates other links with technology, especially when these are drawn as plans and perhaps modelled. There is also scope for links with art in reconstructing your area as it must have been in earlier ages and the things which our ancestors used every day. The spatial distribution and expansion of settlements are central parts of geographical study, as is mapping the results of such studies.

Analysing census data and the distribution of buildings and building materials, and then expressing the findings in the form of appropriate graphs and charts, clearly has relevance to the 'Handling Data' attainment target in mathematics.

In English, listening is an important and useful skill, and there is plenty of scope for this when using oral history. The same requirement to distinguish between fact and opinion is important in both English and history, and oral history is also likely to extend awareness of dialect and vocabulary specific to particular age groups, communities, occupations, etc. The changing use of language is also reflected by the study of newspapers at different dates.

Such links, while important, will be fairly obvious to experienced teachers, and as some would be common to several sources, it has been decided not to list them separately in every chapter, but to draw attention here to the opportunities which exist.

Our chosen sources

The possible list of historical records is huge. The matrix on page 7 shows the ones we are going to describe. But there are many others (see Chapter 13): you probably know of surviving records in your own area which fall outside the range we cover.

For ease of reference, each chapter deals with a separate historical document or other kind of source, in alphabetical order. This does not mean, however, that they should be used in isolation. It is much more likely that several will be combined as part of an investigation. Thus in practice, you may use census returns, directories, old maps and the buildings in the street to answer questions about the past.

We have made our choice for three reasons.

❏ The sources we describe are the most widespread across the country

❏ The documents quoted are usually suitable for photocopying for use in the classroom.

❏ Experience has shown that these are among the simplest to use with young children.

There are many other sources, but some places are particularly rich in local records of all kinds. Your library or record office will be able to tell you about these. The ideas in this book may help you to think of ways of using these other sources.

Curricula in Wales, Northern Ireland and Scotland

The requirements of the History National Curriculum in Wales and Northern Ireland are little different from those in England. Some varied terminology is used, and of course Welsh and Irish history contain different events. Nevertheless, the provision of a Local History unit is made, so our approaches should still be of help.

The Scottish Curriculum is based on an entirely different framework. Teachers in Scotland also have to satisfy the underlying need to provide local examples to flesh out general history, however, so although the Units we describe are different, many of the ideas we describe would still be useful.

Copyright

Much of the material we describe takes the form of documents produced more than 70 years ago. However, from your routine work preparation you will know that any work still in Copyright (that means all written, drawn and printed work - including your own - produced less than 70 years ago), often may not be copied without permission. Sometimes a fee must be paid.

When you obtain copies of source material for your class use, you may be asked by the supplier to sign a form giving details of your use, and this may have a fee attached. We cannot give any formal assurance that you will never have to pay, it depends on what you want to copy. You may freely copy any writing by an author who has been dead for more than 70 years; but the Ordnance Survey allows copying of maps after 50 years. Permission is often required from Record Offices, however, to copy other material regardless of its age.

The Copyright Act allows you to make one copy of most things for your own study. Permission and the attendant fee partly depend on the importance of what you want to copy to the original document. (Thus, if you wish to copy most of a book, the publisher would not unreasonably feel that you should be buying the whole book rather than making a copy).

As a general rule of thumb, the following notes may be helpful:

a) It is probably all right to copy up to 250 words of text.

b) For over 250 words, (or over 5% of a book) write for permission first.

c) Permission should be obtained for copying more than a very small part of a poem or piece of music.

d) Government publications require permission, but allowances are better.

e) Illustrations and tables also require permission.

f) Ordnance Survey maps: five copies or more (of A4 size) need permission. Most LEAs have a licence from the Ordnance Survey which allows schools to make multiple copies of such A4 extracts; but schools should check first.

Using information technology in local history

Much of what the historian does is concerned with the examination and interrogation of evidence. This is investigated and analysed, and thus Information Technology (IT) has much to offer the history teacher. This is especially true of those topics which feature local history and local evidence. Moreover, the use of IT can help pupils develop an enthusiasm for history, thus enhancing their knowledge, understanding and appreciation of the past.

In many situations involving the study of local history, IT provides children with a powerful and easily accessible tool with which they can investigate local evidence. Indeed, the computer, with its ability to handle and manipulate large quantities of information, allows pupils to investigate much greater quantities of evidence than would otherwise be possible. This is not to suggest that the use of the computer should replace the traditional skills of the local historian. Rather, IT can complement and develop these skills further.

However, the use of IT enables pupils to move beyond the simple interpretation of local material. They can use computers to investigate and analyse historical evidence in a variety of ways, and reach conclusions based on their examination of the available data. IT provides children with opportunities to progress from specific enquiries to generalisations, and to form and test hypotheses – in fact, to engage in real historical research.

As well as using the computer to investigate historical sources, children can also be involved in the process of transcribing historical material into a form suitable for manipulation by computer. This can involve pupils in sorting, classifying and selecting evidence. The computer is in effect helping pupils to appreciate both the strengths and weaknesses of historical sources. With IT, pupils can handle considerable amounts of data quickly. Local history provides interesting data, so putting the two together enables children to begin to think scientifically.

In addition to providing an easily accessible tool for interrogating and manipulating historical evidence, the computer is also a powerful and exciting means of promoting empathy and realistic decision-making. Simulation programs can enhance a local study, and IT provides teachers with a means of putting children in situations that would be difficult to recreate by other means.

Pupils frequently find the use of a computer to be exciting and highly motivating. Information technology can harness this, and help develop an interest in and enthusiasm for the study of local history.

Summary

❐ Have your chosen history plan in mind.

❐ Look at our matrix of coverage.

❐ Skim-read a chapter to note our layout:

BACKGROUND	WHERE?	HSUs
ACTIVITIES	IT	PROBLEMS.

❐ Be aware of possible copyright difficulties.

So now, bearing in mind that history comes alive when you are studying your own locality, see what riches your area has to offer!

Relevance of chapters to National Curriculum Study Units

Chapter headings	History Study Unit titles					
	KS 1		Tudors	Victorian Britain	Britain since 1930 (KS2)	Local History (KS2)
		Medieval Realms	Making of the UK (Crown, etc)	Expansion Trade and Industry	Second World War	Local examples (KS3)
Artefacts	✔	✔	✔	✔	✔	✔
Buildings	✔	✔	✔	✔	✔	✔
Census returns				✔		✔
Directories				✔	✔	✔
Inventories			✔	✔		✔
Maps and air photographs		✔	✔	✔	✔	✔
Newspapers				✔	✔	✔
Oral history	✔				✔	✔
Parish registers			✔	✔		✔
Photographs and pictures	✔	✔	✔	✔	✔	✔
School logbooks				✔		✔

2 Artefacts

The variety of artefacts

Artefacts are objects made by people. They vary in size and complexity from something as small and apparently simple as a safety pin to one as large and complex as a Lancaster bomber. Not all artefacts made in the past have survived and many of those which have are broken or fragmentary. Even the most fragmentary or mundane artefact, however, can be made to reveal a vast range of information, provided we examine it closely and ask the right questions of it. In so doing, children will be encouraged to develop a range of skills and concepts which are particularly applicable to the study of history, but have relevance across the curriculum.

Artefacts used to develop an aspect of local history can come from a wide spectrum of time. Almost any artefact dating from the Roman period to the 1970s (or even 1990s) can be relevant.

Artefacts may be selected to provide evidence for a local study for several reasons.

❒ They were found locally, although they may have been manufactured outside the local area. Pottery, jewellery, weapons or other artefacts from a local Saxon cemetery could be used to provide unique evidence of life in the locality at that time.

❒ They were used locally, but manufactured elsewhere, e.g. a cast iron saucepan made in the West Midlands but used by the wife of a miner in a Durham colliery village. In such circumstances the artefacts may be no different from countless others found throughout Britain, but it is their local associations that invest them with significance for the study of history at a local level.

❒ They were made locally but had widespread use throughout Britain and perhaps even further afield, e.g. the Whitby jet jewellery so fashionable in the Victorian and Edwardian periods.

❒ They were made and used locally, e.g. the products of an 18th century brick kiln which provide the only evidence of that industry.

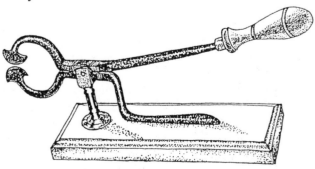

Fig. 2.1 *Nineteenth century sugar nippers*

To children using such objects, local history is made real and tangible when they know the place where the artefact was found, used or made, and perhaps even the person who used it. Objects with local associations can also invest national history with local relevance and hence a greater sense of reality. To children at school in Abingdon, musket balls from the skeletons of soldiers killed in the town during the Civil War have an historical quality far greater than the thousands of other musket balls found scattered throughout museums.

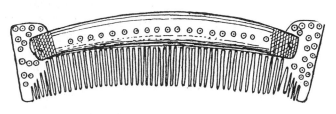

Fig. 2.2 Saxon bone comb

WHERE?

Finding artefacts

Artefacts made or used by people in your locality in this century are readily available from a variety of sources. Your school may contain things used by earlier generations of children, ranging from desks with holes for an inkwell to old sweet tins from a local manufacturer now used for storing drawing pins. Your own home or those of the children are good sources of everyday objects used by previous generations. Members of your community may also have objects with local associations which they are prepared to lend or bring into school and talk about.

Schools intending to set up their own permanent collection of artefacts should take advice from their nearest registered museum about appropriate methods of documenting and caring for the objects they collect, all of which are unique pieces of evidence of life in the past. Your local museum may be able to help in identifying artefacts in your collection, or those loaned to the school, and in obtaining more information about the circumstances in which they were made or used.

A more comprehensive collection of artefacts with local associations will usually be found in the local museum, where children may also have the opportunity to see a range of them displayed in the context in which they were originally used. If your local museum does not have objects relevant to your study they should be able to advise you where such things may be seen.

Many museums have educational facilities and can provide information and advice about the use of objects. The staff of museums and some historic houses may be able to offer activities using artefacts with specifically local associations, ranging from handling sessions to problem-solving and role-playing activities. You may even be fortunate enough to have a museum loan service in your area from which you can borrow a collection of objects related to a local study. Contact your local museum or LEA to find out whether such a service exists and whether the material has local associations.

HSUs
Artefacts and the National Curriculum

At KS1, the use of artefacts is particularly valuable in providing concrete, tactile evidence of change in aspects of everyday life such as clothes, washing, cooking, cleaning, lighting, heating, shops, transport and entertainment.

At KS2, artefacts provide the majority of evidence for the way of life of the Roman, Anglo-Saxon or Viking settlers in your locality. Aspects of urban and rural life in the Tudor period may well be evidenced by local domestic artefacts. There are plenty of artefacts to provide evidence about most aspects of Victorian life, and artefacts can similarly provide a major resource for the study of Britain since 1930. The use of artefacts can also be relevant to the study of local history.

At KS3, artefacts may be used to provide local evidence for many aspects of domestic life, the economy, trade, transport, communications and culture.

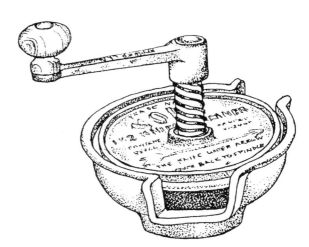

Fig. 2.3 *Knife polisher*

ACTIVITIES
Using artefacts

To use artefacts effectively in the study of any aspect of history, teachers need to select their examples with care. Objects for local studies need not be rare, and often the greatest value comes from items which were in common use, but which can provide information specific to a particular locality.

Looking at, handling and exploring are the first steps in interrogating an object. Avoid starting with closed questions like "What is this?" or "How old is it?" Instead start with questions based on first-hand examination of the object:

Physical features

❑ Texture, smell, colour, shape, size.

❑ What is it made of? Man-made material or natural material?

❑ Is it composed of more than one material?

❑ Is it complete or only a part?

❑ Has it been altered or adapted?

❏ Are there signs of wear?

❏ Does it have any inscription on it, such as the name of the maker, user, or a trademark or patent number?

Construction

Was it made:

❏ by hand?

❏ by machine?

❏ in separate pieces?

❏ by one person or several?

How was it fixed together?

Using the evidence obtained from questions such as these you can then move on to pose more theoretical questions, the answers to which should be based on the evidence available.

Fig. 2.4 *Flat iron*

Function

❏ For what purpose was it made?

❏ Has its use been changed? (Objects made for one purpose may subsequently be used for another: the favourite old mug which, having lost its handle, becomes a pen pot).

Design

❏ Is it well designed for the function it served?

❏ Are the materials appropriate?

❏ Did it do the job efficiently?

❏ Was it decorated, and if so, how and why?

Value

❏ What was its value to the maker, the user and to us today?

❏ What makes an item valuable? (Monetary value, sentimental value, historical value).

Finally one can ask what this object tells us about the period or place we are studying, in the light of the answers obtained from examining it.

Assessing the evidence

Artefacts, like documents, are sources of evidence which have to be interpreted to give us information about the past. The value and reliability of the evidence, and of its interpretation, have to be questioned in the same way as with a document. If you have only one rush light holder known to have been used in a local house-hold, can you be certain that it was typical of that period in your locality? You should always be aware of the potential for bias and inaccuracy.

IT

Handling artefacts by computer

The study of artefacts provides an excellent opportunity for the use of "branching" type programs or what are sometimes called expert systems or binary trees. These are a variation of the data handling programs where children interrogate and analyse evidence or data; they fall into the information retrieval category and provide an opportunity for children to "teach" the computer the important and essential features of a number of objects (or artefacts). Once children have created the "expert system" others can use it to identify an object in front of them.

Use of this type of program is rather similar to the game of "20 Questions" where the aim is to identify an object by asking questions, the answer to which is always "yes" or "no". Similarly, in creating a binary tree, children phrase questions, the answer to which will again be "yes" or "no". When other children use the tree they will be asked a series of questions by the computer and, when all the choices are eliminated, the object in front of them will be identified.

Whilst children find it fun to use a binary tree to identify an object, the real learning and understanding comes from setting up an expert system of their own. In creating a tree, children will inevitably need to examine the objects or artefacts to be classified very carefully. Perhaps they will need to carry out additional research to find out more about the artefact in question and so to be able to distinguish one artefact from another very clearly in their own minds. Finally, they must phrase a clear and concise question to which another user will be able to answer "yes" or "no" about any artefact in the collection without any confusion or misunderstanding. In setting up a binary tree, children will be developing skills of observation and classification as well as planning their work in an organised way. They will also be developing language skills and learning more about the objects or artefacts they are studying.

When children are creating a binary tree, careful planning and organisation will make the task easier and will result in a tree which is better constructed and more efficient to use. Children should probably start with a small number of artefacts to classify initially, perhaps eight to ten; they can add more objects to their tree later.

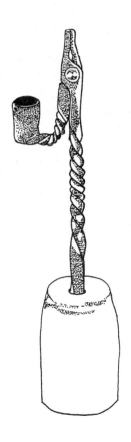

Fig. 2.5 Rushlight or candle holder

Children should also try to think of questions which will divide the group of objects roughly in half at each stage. In this way the tree is balanced and efficient to use.

As well as the use of "branching" type programs to enhance the understanding of artefacts, there are a number of archaeological simulation programs available, which can contribute to children's understanding of artefacts. In addition, teachers might also consider computer aided design (CAD) or "paint" type programs. With these, children can construct or draw very accurate representations of artefacts. Many of the more powerful word processing and desk-top publishing programs available in schools will allow children to combine their CAD or paint type images into a written account of their investigations.

Possible difficulties using artefacts

One of the key problems associated with objects is getting access to them. Everyday objects associated with your area will usually be found in local museum collections, but rarer items may be in more distant specialist museums as part of regional or national collections. Because they are rare or fragile, many objects cannot be handled, but children who have been shown how to analyse artefacts can still obtain a considerable amount of information from careful observation of items in a display.

We all see artefacts differently. Our cultural experiences may influence the way we view them, as will existing knowledge and experience. Gender may also colour our approach. A flat iron may be dismissed by a boy as a "girl's object", failing to see that this particular iron was not intended for domestic use but was a vital tool in the local tailoring trade.

Children may dismiss apparently familiar objects as having nothing to offer – "It's a saucepan. We all know what a saucepan is" – and thus fail to recognise the additional information and ideas that can be gained from it. Why does it have such a long handle? Why is it black on the outside? Is the name on the handle that of a local foundry?

3 Buildings

BACKGROUND
Features of buildings

Apart from its physical identity (i.e. where it is, what it is called) the most obvious evidence of your local place will be its buildings. With the other features such as canals, boundary ditches, walls and field patterns, they each say something about your area at a particular period.

Survivals from particular periods may be few and much altered over time. They will certainly not reflect the whole range of original structures. For example, a row of Tudor buildings in your High Street will have been merchants' houses and workshops, but the tiny wattle and daub homes of ordinary people will have long since been replaced.

Even so, general conclusions can be drawn from buildings that survive. When your pupils study maps, directories, censuses etc., they 'get to know' individual families and individuals from the past. If you can find the buildings these people lived in and actually look at them (or pictures of them), they suddenly become real. Indeed, the buildings can help to tell us how they lived; how well off the community was; and what materials were available to build with. Moreover, written records tied in with what pupils can see, give an idea of what daily life must have been like.

The range of useful buildings throughout history is wide. People took whatever materials they could afford, to produce the most secure and weatherproof structures possible, for a multitude of uses (see Table 3.1). This chapter concentrates mainly on the outside of houses and similar buildings, since we haven't space to cover everything.

Local builders have been constrained by various conditions. If we know how to read these, today's buildings can help us to investigate those influencing factors.

Materials

Stone or lack of it (for foundations, walls and roofs), soil type and condition (affecting brick quality and colour), and timber (for house frames), reflect not only availability and convenience of use, but cost and fashion.

Space

When populations are low and poor, their villages and houses are small. At first, people expand their houses to fill every bit of space available to them (for example, overhanging first floors, 'jettying', and infilling by building in their yards and gardens). As numbers grow, communities spread. But houses only get larger as wealth increases.

Table 3.1 Useful buildings at various dates

Date range	Age	Buildings etc
To 3000BC[1]	Paleolithic/"Stone age"	Caves. Temporary shelters of local materials [2]
3000 to 1500BC	Bronze age	Stone or timber ring houses. Wattle and daub. Mines. PreChristian temple sites; burial mounds.[3] Timber long houses[4]
1500BC to AD1	Iron age	Sophistication of the above. Settlements
1 to 400	Roman	Town layouts. Markets. Villas and settlements. Bridges. Mills
400 to 1000	"Dark ages"/Saxons/Vikings	Settlements. Long houses. Churches. Boundary ditches
1000 to 1500	Norman/Medieval	Brick chimneys. Defensive walls (timber, stone) and ditches. Managed woods. Cathedrals
1500 to 1750	Early modern	Timber scarcer. Brick buildings. Early industrial buildings. Neoclassical
1750 to 1900	Modern industrial (Victorian)	Turnpikes. Canals, railways. Town expansions.[5] Factories
1900 to 1950	Recent (Edwardian/George V/VI)	Town planning. Suburbia. Cars and their requirements
1950 on	Today (post industrial)	Rebuilding plans. Tower blocks. Concrete and glass. Brick.

Notes for Table 3.1

This table is divided into arbitrary periods, roughly reflecting: ways of life which affected buildings; and building traditions and materials.

1. For several reasons, precise dating is impossible. Different parts of the UK will have developed at different speeds in different periods. Local conditions often overrode changes elsewhere. Changes do not necessarily mean that older methods did not continue alongside new ones.

2. Local materials. Apart from the obvious presence or absence of suitable stone, geological make-up of the soil and climatic conditions vary the materials available for building.

3. Geological evidence shows some stones were moved 200 km or so to Stonehenge from the Prescelli Hills, saying much for ritual/ theological needs as well as early resourcefulness.

4. There is written evidence from this period of widespread movement of timber in bulk, with journeys of several hundred miles by land or sea.

5. By about 1800, less than half the population of the UK was involved in agriculture; and by 1851 more than half the population lived in towns.

Economics

Children should think about who lived in the houses that survive. If the rule is: the wealthier the family, the stronger and larger its buildings, then most of today's surviving houses probably belonged to the richest people. Churches too reflect wealth of their patrons and congregations. This was especially so at times when souls could be saved by giving alms and building churches.

Table 3.2 Changes (very approximate) in a market town at various dates

Characteristic	Medieval	Tudor	Victorian	Modern	Note
Population	1500	3000	5000	25,000	1
Number of families	250	650	1000	7500	
Income (average labourer)	£6	£12	£24	£10,000	
Subsistence	←——→				2
Labourer to lord	←——→				
Money for labour	←————————————→				
Craft income	←——————————————————→				
Factory income			←——————————————→		
Food	Self grown	Self grown bought	Self grown bought	bought	3
Bread price (1990 index)		1d (0.25p)	3d (1p)	(10s) 50p	
Transport	Walk	Walk	Walk/rail	Bus/rail/car	
	carter/horse	carter/horse	carter/stage canal/horse/ coach/cycle	(motor) cycle	
Education	Church	Dame schools Grammar schls	Board schools Literacy grows Rising leaving age	Universal	
Houses	Wattle/daub etc.	Wattle/daub etc.	Brick back to back terrace tenements	High rise flats estate semis terraces	
Rooms/family	1	1-3	4	5-6	
Public buildings	Churches etc. Religious buildings Mills/hospitals	Guildhalls/ markets Schools	Town halls Rail/canal buildings Factories	Supermarkets/ Office blocks	

Notes for Table 3.2

1. The figures given are rounded averages, derived by comparing population 'behaviour' of a number of provincial towns. The single figures given throughout the table must only be taken as the roughest of generalisations.

2. The arrows show rough date ranges

3. Prices varied enormously year from year because of poor harvests (bad weather, diseased crops etc.). Bread was home-made in most rural houses, so the figures given tend to be from town bakers. Loaves varied in size anyway. The data given are averaged from several sources. The figures in this row are particularly difficult to check and, partly for this reason, the medieval information is omitted.

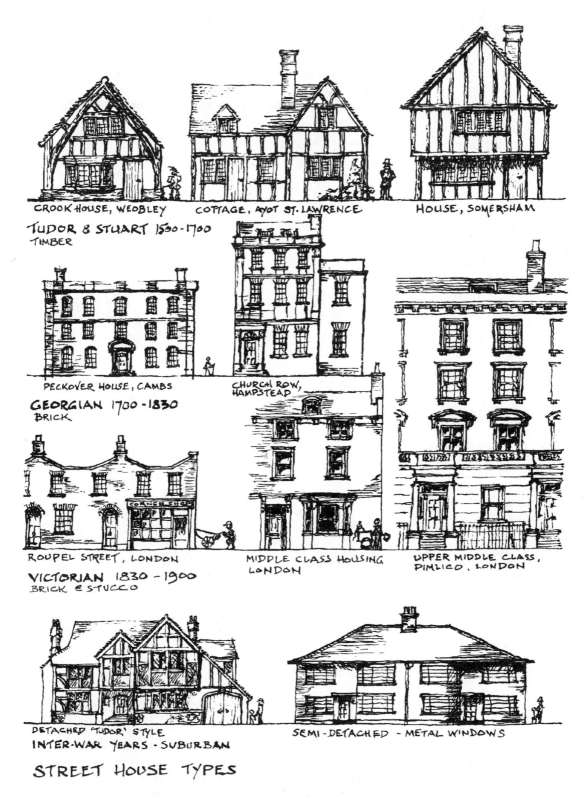

CROOK HOUSE, WEOBLEY   COTTAGE, AYOT ST. LAWRENCE   HOUSE, SOMERSHAM

TUDOR & STUART 1500-1700
TIMBER

PECKOVER HOUSE, CAMBS   CHURCH ROW, HAMPSTEAD

GEORGIAN 1700-1830
BRICK

ROUPEL STREET, LONDON   MIDDLE CLASS HOUSING LONDON   UPPER MIDDLE CLASS, PIMLICO, LONDON

VICTORIAN 1830-1900
BRICK & STUCCO

DETACHED 'TUDOR' STYLE   SEMI-DETACHED - METAL WINDOWS
INTER-WAR YEARS - SUBURBAN

STREET HOUSE TYPES

Fig. 3.1A Features which help to date houses (You may photocopy this figure for class use.)

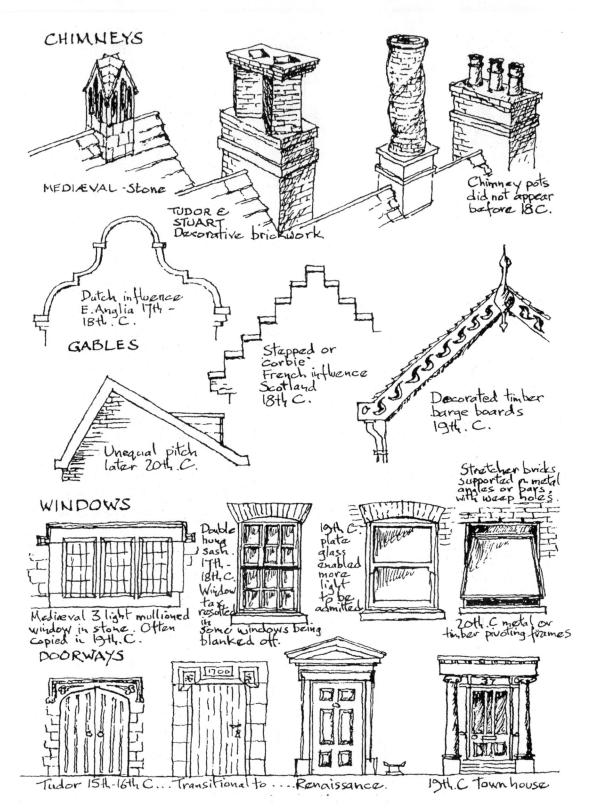

Fig. 3.1B *Features which help to date houses (You may photocopy this figure for class use.)*

Outside influence

Kings or governments often imposed rules which builders had to obey. Taxes influenced size, location and style.

Table 3.2 shows some approximate relationships between different time periods for working class people in a (theoretical) country town. If the trends are as the table shows, what we can see today in local buildings is surrogate evidence for some of these other conditions.

Building types

Domestic, trade and public buildings developed in style and materials over the ages. For typical changes in (housing) materials see Table 3.1; and for a guide to dating buildings by style, see Figure 3.1 and Table 3.3.

Religious architecture developed from monolithic structures, like standing stones, evolving through burial chambers to the soaring churches and cathedrals like the two modern cathedrals in Liverpool. Figure 3.2 shows how church architecture changed over time.

Early traders made and sold their products in markets and from their houses. Shop and workshop development followed domestic architecture. Specialist buildings evolved, such as mills, forges etc; and market stalls gradually became fixed shops.

Communal life created a need for structures such as guildhalls, inns, hospitals, lockups and similar public buildings.

What can buildings tell us?

When we walk round, what can the surviving buildings reveal about the past? Can we draw conclusions from our one small area of the UK, and make useful generalisations about the past? It is not so much what our surroundings can reveal, as deciding how to unravel what is there: here is a detective story where everything is a clue! The following sections, used in parallel with other sources – like directories, censuses, maps, inventories etc. – may help to explain what buildings can tell us about the people who lived in them.

WHERE?

Finding buildings
a) Printed records

Your local library and record office will have descriptions of listed buildings. These are often collected together by age. They will include maps, or refer closely to them.

The same libraries will hold the Victoria County History volumes (which series describes most areas), Pevsner's *Buildings of England* and other printed books covering your area. A very quick scan of these reveals descriptions of the most important buildings in the place. Modern guide books help to locate the survivors.

Local museums and art galleries (as well as record offices and libraries) also hold pictures and plans of important buildings. These often include useful interior photographs.

b) Fieldwork

Walking round your town or village centre, or the locality of your school will reveal that many building ages are represented. See the ACTIVITIES section on producing a local buildings map.

The following sections provide help in dating and describing buildings, to help build a picture of what your area was like.

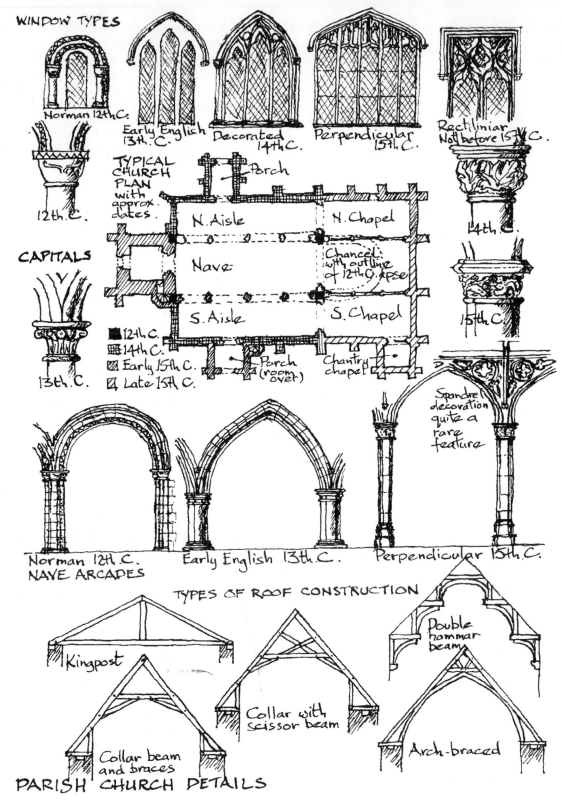

WINDOW TYPES

Norman 12th C.

Early English 13th. C.

Decorated 14th C.

Perpendicular 15th C.

Rectiliniar Not before 15th C.

CAPITALS

12th. C.

13th. C.

14th. C.

15th C.

TYPICAL CHURCH PLAN with approx. dates.

Porch

N. Aisle   N. Chapel

Nave   Chancel with outline of 12th C. apse

S. Aisle   S. Chapel

■ 12th C.
▦ 14th C.
▨ Early 15th C.
▧ Late 15th C.

Porch (room over)   Chantry chapel

Norman 12th. C. NAVE ARCADES

Early English 13th. C.

Perpendicular 15th. C.

Spandrel decoration quite a rare feature

TYPES OF ROOF CONSTRUCTION

Kingpost

Collar beam and braces

Collar with scissor beam

Double hammar beam

Arch-braced

PARISH CHURCH DETAILS

Fig. 3.2 *Features which help to date churches (You may photocopy this figure for class use.)*

Table 3.3 Identifying date ranges for features in buildings

Characteristic	1500	1600	1700	1800	1900	1950	1991
Type		Big houses' main rooms: 1st floor		1775 Canal; 1820 Railway Special housing estates Factories	Cinemas	High rise 1960–80 Large estates Prefabs	
Style		Dutch influence 1650–1750	Neoclassical	Ornate; eg bargeboards Gothick		Glass & concrete	
Bricks	English bond predominates Bricks 2.25" thick; Dark patterns in lighter brick walls Brick chimneys	Flemish bond predominant 1625 Bricks 2.5" thick;	1709 Act (limits use of external wooden frames)	1776 Brick 3" thick Brick imitates stone	1920 stretcher bond (cavity walls) 1920 Damp courses Air bricks: 1920 regular	Weep holes 1950 occasional	
Doors	Vertical planks	Panelled doors	18th C Hinges/knockers/handles/finger plates 18th C Bell pulls 1770s Mortice locks	Early 19th C Numbers on houses 1840 Letterboxes	Bell pushes 1860s Yale locks		
Windows	Unglazed single openings	Small panes: blown glass Several small openings Iron frames	1694 window tax 1851 Sash windows with bars: thick 1750 thinner Sliding sashes		Plate (cast) glass 1930s curved metal bays		
Roofs	1502 Terracotta tiles	Dutch gables	18th C Slate roofs	1860 Shiny glazed tiles			
Floors	Earth/mortar to 19th C	Early 17th C Parquet		Wood block 1788 Plaster		Cork	
Walls			Dado rails Picture (& plate) rails Stucco plaster 18th C imitation stone				
Ceilings				Paper lined	1930s Plasterboard		
Fires	Wood burning Fire dogs andirons	Coal burning Grate with fire basket	Hob grate	Late 18th C Central heating	Gas heating Electric fires		
Stairs			18th C Banisters				

The dates when features first appeared is roughly where words start in the table. If features end at a known date this is also shown.

Materials

Does the geology of your area suggest an abundance of a particular building stone? If so, how many buildings in the particular area you are studying are actually in that material? See Figure 3.3. If not, why not? Did the stone run out? Was it too expensive? Particular building materials may reflect the availability of different transport systems. One good example was the use of Dutch bricks as ballast in ships returning to East Anglia after exporting textiles to the Low Countries.

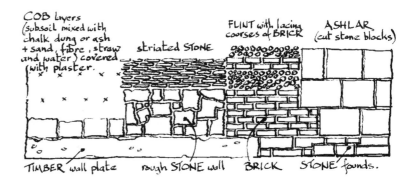

Fig. 3.3 Walls may be made of various materials, but are not often as mixed as this!

Bearing in mind that the best stone will be used first, later buildings had to be built either of poorer quality material, or of good stone from further afield, or of good stone that was more difficult to quarry. You may be able to locate disused stone quarries in your area. (Try large scale maps and directories.)

Are there a lot of brick buildings, perhaps of the 'half-timbered' sort? Look for wooden frames: in half timbered houses the woodwork often matches and the left-hand side of a building often mirrors the right. (How did carpenters achieve this? By making good copies from different pieces of timber? Or by splitting the same piece of timber?) Look for evidence of buildings being crooked because straight wood could not be found; or wood being chosen for particular jobs, such as angles in the building made by using naturally curved timber.

The Victorian middle class liked to imitate their wealthy superiors. Since these mainly lived in ornate, stone mansions, many Victorian houses were highly decorated. Look for carved flowers, faces, shields etc. Bricks were often painted and shaped to imitate the stone-built houses of wealthy neighbours.

BRICK BONDS

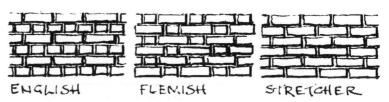

Fig. 3.4

Bricks have been used for many centuries. But the patterns brick-layers use (bonds) are different. Only since the 1920s have houses had to have cavity walls, so brickwork using Stretcher Bond (see Figure 3.4) must either be only one brick thick or be built after 1930.

Only the most menial of buildings (e.g. today's single-storey outhouses) would have single-brick walls (early houses built this way will have been replaced or rebuilt at later dates). So a useful rule is: Stretcher Bond = post 1920s.

See how many different brickwork bonds you can find. (Discuss the limitations to possible patterns vis-a-vis wall strength). Look out for houses with different bond patterns (and brick colours) in its walls: evidence of alterations and extensions.

Roofs are today mainly of tile or slate. Split stone is also used in areas where stone is used for building. (Look for graded tiles: the higher up the roof the smaller the tile. Roofers had different names for each size.)

Thatch used to be much more common, even in buildings now tiled. Thatched roofs had to be sloped more steeply than those of other materials. Why? (Rain and snow are more likely to run quickly off smooth stone/slate/tile than thatch). For obvious reasons, their chimneys had to be set high above the level of the thatch. See Figure 3.5 for one way of deciding if a roof was once thatched.

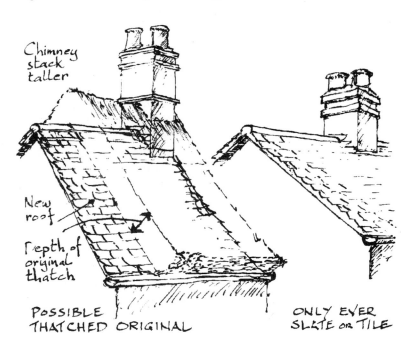

Fig. 3.5 Features that help to identify a roof that was once thatched

Children could draw (or model) the construction of a timber-framed house: sawyers in saw pits; brick kilns; stonemasons laying foundation layers and chimneys; etc.

Features

There are many books on architectural styles through the ages, and it is not possible in this book to describe the huge variety one may meet round the country. Nevertheless, a few individual hints may be helpful.

Windows

Glass was expensive in the past, so window areas were small. From the 15th to the 18th centuries, small mullioned windows (i.e. with vertical bars) prevailed. Eighteenth and early 19th century windows had small, square panes; sash windows were introduced, with wooden bars dividing them. Earlier Georgian windows had thicker bars; later ones much more delicate. See Figure 3.6.

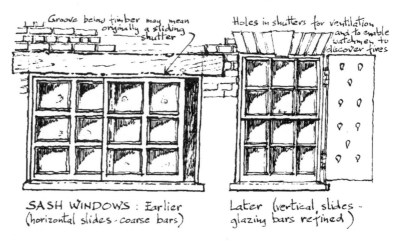

Fig. 3.6 Windows and shutters

Today's prized circular 'bulls-eye' panes were originally the central part of spun-glass sheets. Since these gave less light, our ancestors valued them least!

Not until the mid Victorian period were large windows made, after the method of plate glass manufacture was developed.

'Weavers' windows' date from when people worked at home, their looms often being sited upstairs. So, in the pre-factory age, look for rows of windows of two or three normal window widths, especially at first floor level.

Between 1696 and 1851 a tax was in force on the number of windows in houses. To save money, many were bricked up. From 1825, houses with fewer than eight windows were exempt.

Chimneys

Until the 13th century there were no chimneys, only holes in the roof. These were formalised into vents, still sited in the middle of the building. The recently renovated Barley Hall, in Coffee Yard, off Stonegate, York, contains a fine example.

From the 1400s brick chimneys were built, even in stone buildings, since hot bricks do not crack as readily as stone. Chimney pots only appeared widely after 1750. Fireplaces were moved to the side walls to get out of people's way in the living space, but this was a bad idea on outside walls because of the heat loss. So other rooms were built around the chimney where possible. Fireplaces were added to upper storeys. Chimney stacks became wide to give access for sweeps. At ground level, bulges at the base of chimney stacks were often ovens.

Finishes

Original wooden frames were often not meant to be seen. Look at the surface. Nail heads were used as as keys for plaster but today perhaps only the holes will show. House fronts were rendered to stop water rotting the timber and wind from blowing through the walls (see Figure 3.7).

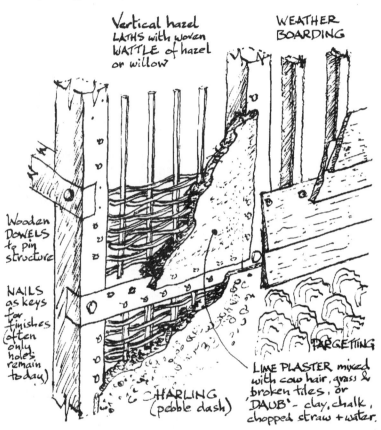

Fig. 3.7 Timber framed walls: make-up and finishes

Local materials were used. Bricks infilled some timber frames. Added protection was provided by tiles, especially on the weather side; overlapping wooden planks (weatherboarding, often tarred); plaster (sometimes decorated 'pargetting', and usually painted); or cement. The latter often had stones embedded in the coat as added protection, either through traditional 'harling' (the stones were *hurled* at wet cement) or more modern 'pebble-dash'.

Buildings other than houses
Public buildings: trade

Market stalls developed into shops. Look for trader street names near market places, such as Butcher Row, Tanner Street, Shambles (where meat was butchered and sold), and so on. Local groups formed guilds, with market houses, guildhalls and town halls for communal use. Often these were imposing reminders of a place's past wealth. Look at the chapters on 'Directories' and 'Census returns' for activities involving trades.

Inns

Look for archways leading to coaching-inn courtyards. Inns were used for public meeting places, carters' collecting points and transport stages, as well as for ostlery, refreshment and accommodation. Later, what were blacksmiths' shops became garages, and mews houses (originally where falcons 'mewed', that is, moulted) changed from being mere service roads into storage garages, and indeed desirable residences.

Pounds, lock-ups

Pounds for lost animals may survive only as street names. But many lock-ups survive, taking a variety of forms. Pillories, stocks etc. are sometimes to be found in churchyards, as well as museums.

Transport buildings

Buildings were carefully planned and built as the canals and railways spread. Company styles were common to all the buildings along their routes. Sometimes the railways have disappeared, but recognisable buildings remain.

Tunnels and bridges involved huge works, with specialist craftsmen temporarily encamped around structures as they were built. Typical examples were families of brickmakers, who used the spoil from tunnel digs to make the bricks of which the tunnels were lined; and carpenters who made the frameworks which were moved along into the tunnel as it progressed. See Figure 3.8. If works like these were done in your area in a census year, a good study could be designed.

Fig. 3.8 Tunnel building in principle. Many trades were involved and the workforce often ran into thousands. The work was dangerous: Woodhead Tunnel in the Peak District, claimed 28 dead, and 200 serious injuries in 450 accidents

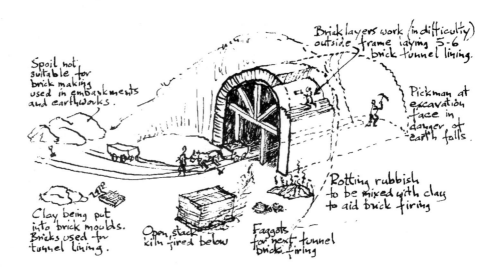

Farms

Barns, byres etc evolved into specialised buildings (original cruck designs were divided into bays, each the width of four tethered oxen). Doorways set centrally in the side of a barn suggest an original threshing floor inside. When the door was open, to let the wind blow husks away during winnowing, a removable sill (the 'spurting board') stopped the grain escaping.

Churches, cathedrals, castles

As we have stated, we have no space to cover all buildings, inside and out. Figure 3.2 gives a taste of some changes in church architecture, but the reader is referred to the many books which cover these important historical sources.

Miscellaneous

Street paving and street lighting appeared in towns from the early 19th century. Tarmacadam roads, appeared in 1815 in Bristol; gas lighting was first used in the 1820s; and electricity in the 1880s.

Signposts were often set at a height to be read from horseback.

House street numbers were not recorded until the mid 19th century in most towns.

People in buildings

The materials used to build houses tell us about the environment in which people lived: the timber used reflects the local woodlands, supplying oak for beams, ash for roof and wall laths and hazel for wattle. Walls made from the local subsoil of clay or chalk were originally mixed with cow dung to provide cob, and cow-hair for plaster.

Inside, ancient roof and wall beams may be blackened by rush-lights and fire smoke. Often, they show evidence of ceiling hooks from which provisions were hung. The under side of ancient wall beams may contain grooves, indicating the use of sliding shutters, before the days of window glass. When glass was expensive, and when the only alternatives were thin sheets of horn etc., the poorer houses would only have had wooden shutters to keep out the weather. Holes in these (and later shutters too) were not just decoration, but also to let in the light; in addition, they enabled the passing watchman to look inside closed buildings at night and be able to see a possible fire through the shutters.

Some buildings have dates on them (on shields over the front door; downpipe hoppers, etc.). These may well be when the building was built; but sometimes people commemorated special family events in this way, and new owners making substantial extensions to the original building may also have added the date. Quite often initials appear on the same places, usually signifying the owner or the builder. Even the name of the house itself is often carved on a stone over the front door. (You may be able to investigate this in the case of Victorian buildings if they coincide with a census. Such names make useful recognition landmarks if you are checking a census on the ground)

HSUs

Buildings and the National Curriculum

At KS1, buildings provide usefully tangible evidence of the past and clearly demonstrate to young children differences from today.

Two approaches may be useful for KS2 and KS3: studying an area in depth, and looking at a particular building to see what it would be like to live there. For KS2 the SU2 *Life in Tudor Times* and SU3a *Victorian Britain* call for the latter approach; at KS3, SU1 *Medieval Realms* and SU2 *Making of the UK* can include the study of homes and styles of living, while buildings of many kinds are an aspect of industrialisation in SU3.

Buildings provide obvious evidence of domestic living conditions at all periods for which they survive (or have been reconstructed), but examples such as tollhouses, railway stations, mills, factories or churches and chapels can illustrate the commercial, industrial or religious perspectives of history, as well as showing technological changes.

Buildings are also a natural starting point for a KS2 Local History Study Unit.

Buildings provide clear evidence of continuity as well as change, and are therefore very useful for illustrating these concepts.

Looking at a street plan, and walking round the place itself, will probably reveal the original centre(s). For the modern centre, study the skyline: the most expensive land tends to support the tallest office blocks. If the parish church is the tallest building, that too often signals the ancient centre; or it may be centred round an important road or river crossing. If there is still no sign of a centre, seek the market area. Towns often began as settlements around a

Using buildings
The town structure

Fig. 3.9 *Site of the medieval market in High Wycombe, Buckinghamshire*

'village green' (in Saxon times), with the central area used as a market space. The evolution from open space to modern built up town centre, via market stalls and semi-permanent shops, often shows up (from street shapes) when you are 'reconstructing' the town centre in this way. See Figure 3.9.

Trying to picture what a place was like in the distant past (in Tudor times, say) begins by establishing how large it was. So try to establish boundaries at different dates.

Later, towns were founded or developed for other specific reasons (railway towns; seaside resorts; university towns; etc.).

Remember that history includes 'now'! We are not only looking at ancient buildings. Indeed, it makes good sense to start the local history survey of your area by studying recent developments. Children understand history best by working backwards from their own time.

Individual buildings

Establishing the age of individual houses and public buildings is what actually links today's building to the past. We can see what size of house supported known families (by reference to Census records, Directories, etc). We can get an idea of lifestyles from domestic house contents and other artefacts; records will also reveal houseowners' wealth (see our chapters on Artefacts and on Inventories). We can even speculate about our ancestors' health, by reference to wells, pumps, overcrowding, sanitation, lighting, damp, heat, etc.

1. Buildings survey

a) On to an outline map, have the children draw the buildings within your chosen area, identifying those from different periods.

b) Mark in the sites of civic buildings, churches, and modern markets. If none of these is obvious, check street names, which may reveal what you seek. (Look for elements like Cheap and Row; and those bearing trade names, like Sheep (or Ship) Street, Horsefair, etc.)

c) Find out from survivals from different periods what your area looked like at different times. (Pictures and photographs as well as fieldwork evidence will help). Who would have lived in buildings like the ones you have found? (Directories may help).

d) Get the children to draw an area that your class researched to show what it must have looked like. Use a surviving real building as the centrepiece of the picture if you can.

2. Building materials

a) Establish what your area's buildings were made of. Find out where the materials might have come from (you might use directories for this). What specialist craftsmen would have had to combine to build them?

b) Find out and draw as many different brickwork patterns (bonds) in house walls as you can. Why is today's 'stretcher bond' used? (Figure 3.10 may help).

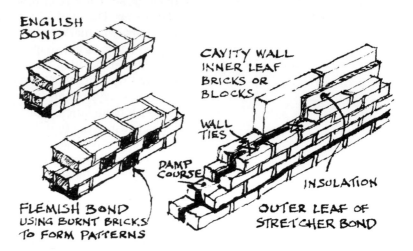

Fig. 3.10 *Brick bonds in use*

c) Look at the roofs in your area (thatched, slated or tiled). Investigate using a model why roofs are better sloped than flat. Why are thatched roofs steeper than slated or tiled ones?

3. Building features

a) Investigate the link between good buildings and health. What measures have people taken through the years to keep out the rain, wind and damp from their houses?

b) Using polythene and wooden blocks, of brick proportions, build some walls of different patterns to combine strength with a flow of air.

c) Draw windows from different periods, showing how they changed. Why is it a good idea for windows to be larger? (Why not build houses entirely of glass?)

d) What architectural features did the Roman and Georgian periods have in common? Using reference books, find comparable features from the two periods.

4. Trade buildings

a) Get the children in groups, to think what special buildings might be needed to do various jobs. (Directories and censuses list occupations; Oral history may be useful). What makes these buildings different from one another? Is there evidence of these in your area now? Can the children find pictures in books?

b) In groups, model or draw special buildings: these could perhaps be combined into a display.

5. Public buildings

a) Have the class find out about local utilities supply in your period (water/gas/lighting)

b) Look at pictures of (or visit) a school dating from your period. How do the school buildings differ from your own school? Can you make a model?

c) Draw (i) an Anglican or Roman Catholic church; (ii) a non-conformist chapel and (iii) a mosque or a synagogue. How do they differ? Draw a window from each.

6. People in buildings

a) Who lived in the buildings in your study area? What did they do in them? Why were they built here and not anywhere else?

b) In groups of four, (representing mother/father/daughter/son) each write a description of his or her typical day spent living or working in the building you are studying. Think about the life of a large number of children living in one small house (compare the Census chapter). Each piece must mention at least two features about the building itself. Put each group of four together as a display of one family's life.

c) Discuss the pros and cons of moving into a new city suburb in the 1880s, bearing in mind that:
(i) Victorian builders made exaggerated claims about their speculative housing developments.
(ii) Brickmakers allowed rubbish to rot on building sites before burning it mixed in with the clay, as they made the bricks for the new estates. The resulting smell and smoke must have been extremely unpleasant!
(iii) Services (like water, gas and transport) may not have been provided until the estate was well established.
(iv) New houses were better than rat-infested slums.
(v) New houses were nearer thc countryside.
(vi) Where were the jobs situated?

7. General

a) When the children look at styles of building through the ages, which ones do they like best? Why? In groups the class can work out and draw or model a house in the style they like best.

b) Build a street of houses, shops, etc. in the period you are studying.

c) Why is each child's own house better than the ones the group described/drew/modelled?

IT

Buildings and data handling

Information technology can be used to enable children to extend their understanding of buildings in their local area relatively easily. There are many data handling programs available and you will know which one(s) your school holds. (National Council for Educational Technology has produced a helpful list of data handling and other programs for use in schools). Using data handling programs, children or teachers can create a data file containing information about local buildings which children can then use to investigate their local community.

Having decided to provide children with the opportunity of using a data handling program to investigate buildings in the local community, teachers will need to consider how to organise the information to be included in the data file. Those who have used such programs will already be familiar with some of the jargon used. Imagine you have decided to collect a range of information about buildings in your area. You would probably decide to lay the information out rather like a table with columns of information such as Main Building Material, Roof Material, Age of Building, Number of Storeys, etc. Such columns of information are referred to as *fields* whilst the information in a row of such a table (the information about each individual building) is referred to as a *record*. If your data file contained the details for 600 buildings it would contain 600 records.

Most data handling programs will ask you to for a field name to be defined for each column of information and this may need to be an abbreviated version of the column headings for your table of information. When you are constructing a data file of local buildings the suggestions in Table 3.4 may be helpful.

Table 3.4 Possible fields in a buildings database

ADDRESS	The address of the building.
NAME	If applicable. This may be especially useful for identifying shops and business premises.
DATE	The approximate date of construction.
AGE	Children can work this out, or spreadsheets and some other types of data handling program will calculate this result for you.
WALLS	The main building material used in the construction of the building.
ROOF	The main roofing material used in the building.
STOREYS	The number of storeys.
USE	Whether the building is residential or used for business. It is possible to use a numeric code to indicate the main use of the building.
TYPE	Whether detached, semi-detached, terraced, flats, offices, etc.

Clearly, teachers and pupils will need to agree beforehand what specific entries will go into each field; a limited range of choices will provide the best opportunities for producing graphical displays of the information where your data handling program has this facility. Thus, for example, you may want to limit the entry in the WALLS field to Brick, Pebble dash, Imitation stone, Rendered, Stone or Timber frame. The entry in the ROOF field might similarly be limited to Clay tile, Concrete tile, Corrugated, Flat, Lead, Pantile, Stone slate, Welsh slate, Thatch, etc. The main materials used in your local area will help you and your children to construct a sensible list of choices.

There are also some data handling programs which will allow you to construct a base map of your local area and plot the records from your data file on to this base map. If you have access to this type of program you will also need to identify each building's location by defining a field to hold the GRID reference.

Once a data file of local buildings has been created, children can investigate this evidence relatively easily. Many data handling programs will produce charts and graphical displays of the data, and thus children can see very easily the range of building and roofing materials used in their local area as well as the relationship between, for example, WALL and ROOF materials. They can also see the number of buildings from particular periods which still survive, as well as particular periods of development in their town or village. If you have access to a data handling program which will plot the buildings on a base map, children can investigate the spatial relationships between different types of building and roofing materials, as well as gaining a feel for how their community has developed over time.

See Figure 3.11 for some typical IT outputs.

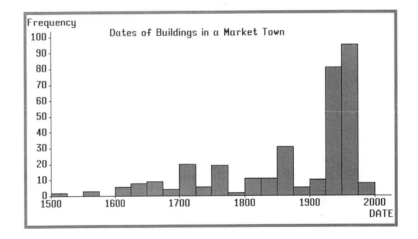

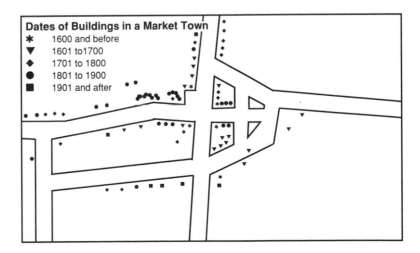

Fig. 3.11A Typical IT outputs

WALLS / DATE	STONE	PEBBLE DASH	BRICK	RENDERED	OTHERS
1500 to 1630	7				4
1630 to 1760	45		1		17
1760 to 1890	21		13	7	22
1890 to 2020	16	77	58	24	19
Others					

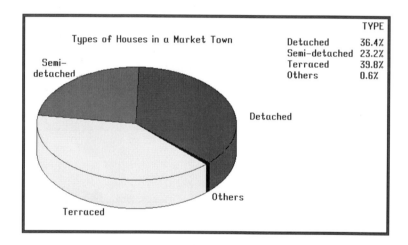

Types of Houses in a Market Town

TYPE	
Detached	36.4%
Semi-detached	23.2%
Terraced	39.8%
Others	0.6%

Field: WALLS	Frequency
BRICK	72
BRICK CLAD	1
PEBBLE DASH	77
RECONSTITUTED STONE	11
RED BRICK	17
RENDERED	31
RENDERED BRICK	3
RENDERED TIMBER FRAME	1
ROUGHCAST	1
RUBBLE	20

Fig. 3.11B Typical IT outputs

PROBLEMS

Possible difficulties using buildings
Survivals

Change

What we see is only what has survived (with pictures of some other buildings). Only the most robust and useful buildings survived. These would tend to have belonged to the wealthy, who could afford good quality, lasting materials.

What you see is likely to have been altered many times since it was built. Compare old photographs with each other and with the same buildings today. Look for evidence of expansions. Study shows that places grow in two ways: through the development of new land around the existing area; and through the development of central areas.

Look for signs of alterations and extensions: different building materials and brickwork bonds, blocked doors and windows, arches wider or narrower than the doors or windows under them.

(Why are changes needed? Houses were knocked together; light was improved; window tax was saved; extra floors were added; etc.)

Some alterations are to keep up with fashion: Georgian fronts were added to much older buildings. For example, look for contrasting walls where accurately laid, square stone or brick fronts, with regular windows contrast with much less formal brickworks etc at the sides and back.

Look for traces of old roof lines showing on end-walls, where an extra storey has been added.

Changes of use

Buildings are often used in different ways over the years: people live in chapels, old shops, inns, mills, barns. Offices may be in converted houses, hotels, warehouses. Hospitals, schools and hotels are often based on earlier buildings. (Why did a mill stop working? Why do people choose to live in barns today?)

Change relates to the use of the area, as well as to individual buildings.

Imitation

Beware modern architectural styles. There are usually elements in the imitation which are not true to the original. Modern imitations contain clues showing they are not original: timbers tend to be square and not rough-edged; brick panels use stretcher bond; there are damp proof courses, etc.

4 Census returns

The early censuses

A census of the population of England and Wales has been taken every ten years since 1801, except for 1941. Until 1841 only the numbers of people in various categories were recorded, not their names or personal details. This was done by Overseers of the Poor and local clergy. The 1841 census was the first one in which an attempt was made to record the name, age and occupation of everyone in the country, although only approximate ages were shown (rounded down to the nearest 5 for those over 15). From 1851 exact ages were asked for, and two important new columns were added to the form stating "Relation to Head of Household" and "Where Born". A further addition in 1891 was the question about the "Number of Rooms Occupied, If Less Than Five".

All personal information in the census remains confidential for 100 years, and so the latest returns we can look at today are those for 1891. The 1901 census will become available in January, 2002.

How the census was made

From 1841 officials called census enumerators were appointed for each district. This was usually an area containing about 200 houses in a town, or, in the country, one where the Enumerator would not have to walk more than 15 miles. Enumerators had to be able to read, write and add up figures, and to have a certain standing in the community. Teachers (among others) were thought to be suitable. Enumerators were always men in the 19th century.

The census has traditionally been taken on a date in March or April. Before the day, the enumerator delivered forms to each household on which the designated "Head" entered the details for everyone present on census night. Those who could not read or write sought help from neighbours or the enumerator himself, and it is easy to imagine that many people were missed, especially in the poorer, crowded areas of Victorian towns. Institutions such as workhouses, hospitals or prisons were recorded separately on special forms.

The enumerator then had to copy all the information from the forms into his enumerator's book, adding up the various totals. These books were eventually returned to the Census Office in London, and it is these "returns" that are consulted by historians today.

Apart from the returns dealt with in this chapter, statistics were produced after each census (including the years after 1891), and these can be used to chart the growth or decline of local populations.

What the census tells us

In general terms the census answers the question "Who lived here in Victorian times?" but it can also help with much more specific inquiries about the sort of people they were, their families, ages, work and where they came from.

Each column has a heading explaining the kind of information included in it (see Table 4.1).

Table 4.1 Columns in a census form

No. of Schedule	The number of this entry in the Enumerator's book – not the number of the house.
Road, Street, etc, and Number or Name of House	Outside big towns few houses were numbered.
Inhabited / Uninhabited	Empty houses were recorded as uninhabited or "Building", i.e. under construction.
Number of Rooms Occupied if Less than Five	This appeared in 1891 for the first time.
Name and Surname of Each Person	
Relation to Head of Family	Helps to identify who everyone in the house was, including servants, visitors, lodgers, etc.
Condition as to Marriage	Married, single, widow or widower.
Age	In separate columns for males and females.
Rank, Profession or Occupation	What work people did, or whether they were at school, paupers or of independent means.
Employer, Employee or Neither	First included in 1891
Where Born	The county and parish (from 1851)
Deaf, Dumb, Blind, Lunatic, Imbecile or Idiot	Probably not completed accurately, and the last three must have been difficult to distinguish

WHERE?

Finding census returns

The original enumerators' returns for the whole country are kept at the Public Record Office in London, but they have been transferred onto microfilm or microfiche and will be available locally in this form. You will find them at your archive office, county library or local studies library if there is one. Copies can be obtained in the form of printouts of each page. There are usually 25 names per page, except in 1851 (20) and 1891 (30).

HSUs

Census returns and the National Curriculum

KS2: Census returns are obviously relevant to the SU on *Victorian Britain*, or to a Local History SU.

KS3: They contain important evidence about industrial change, the growth of towns and living conditions providing a local context for aspects of SU3, *Britain 1750–c.1900*. Census returns provide very good opportunities for developing the skills of understanding and extracting information from a historical source. This leads on to analysing and presenting it in a variety of ways, all of which relates to the Key Element called Organisation and Communication, as well as making use of mathematical skills (handling data) and information technology.

Using census returns
Which census?

The size of the study area

Getting started

Six dates are available, 1841-1891. 1841 contains less detail and so is not often used in school. All of the remaining ones are suitable and there are various reasons for choosing a particular year. It is always worth considering purely practical things like how easy it is to read the handwriting, which varies from year to year. You may wish to link your work to a special event like the Great Exhibition of 1851 or Queen Victoria's Jubilee in 1887, or the opening of your school, in which case you will choose the census nearest to that. If you are looking at the area around your school and you are in the suburbs of a town, the choice of census may be governed by the date at which that part of town was developed. It is a very good idea to relate the work on census returns to other types of source material, especially the early editions of the Ordnance Survey 25 inch maps, which usually date from the 1870s or 1880s. A quite different approach is to select two years and make a comparison between them, observing changes over time.

The projects suggested here can be carried out by children studying just a handful of households (say three or four census pages), or a much larger area like a whole village or part of a town. It depends on the objectives of the study, the ability of the children, the time available and the way the work is organised – as a whole class project or a smaller group activity. A small sample is much easier to manage for young children who may be tackling census returns for the first time. The historical skills that are developed through census work can certainly be learned on a quite small sample. If the nature of the inquiry makes a larger sample essential, several small groups can share the work and pool their findings.

If children are using the census for the first time, it will be helpful to let them become familiar with the layout of the document and the sort of information it contains through a simple introductory exercise, which will also give them a little practice in reading the writing. Working in pairs, with a single census page, let them choose one household and see what they can find out about those people

❐ How many people in the house?

❐ Who is the head?

❐ Are all the people one family?

❐ How many children are there?

❐ What are the children's names?

❐ How old are they?

❐ What work does the head do?

❐ What work does his wife do?

❐ Where was his wife born?

27   Page 7

Administrative County of *Gloucestershire*
Civil Parish of *St Philip & Jacob*   Municipal Borough of *Bristol*   Municipal Ward of *Bristol*   Urban Sanitary District of *Bristol*   Parliamentary Borough or Division of *South Bristol*   Ecclesiastical Parish or District of *St Philip & Jacob*

The undermentioned Houses are situate within the Boundaries of the —

No. of Schedule	ROAD, STREET, &c., and No. or NAME of HOUSE	HOUSES Inhabited	HOUSES Uninhabited	HOUSES Building	NAME and Surname of each Person	RELATION to Head of Family	CONDITION as to Marriage	AGE last Birthday Male	AGE last Birthday Female	PROFESSION or OCCUPATION	Employer	Employed	Neither employer nor employed	WHERE BORN	If Deaf-and-Dumb, Blind, Lunatic, Imbecile or Idiot
49	4 Charlotte St	1		4	George Baggins	Head	M	37		Boot maker		X		Gloucestershire–Bristol	
					Elizabeth do	Wife	M		39					do	
					Edward do	Son	S					X		do	
					Florence do	Daur			15					do	
					Louisa do	Daur			11	Scholar				do	
					Alice do	Daur			9	Scholar				do	
					Annie do	Daur			2					do	
50	9 John St	1		4	Benjamin Horner	Head	M	55		Engine Driver		X		Monmouth	
					John do	Wife	M		47	Boot Maker		X			
					Joseph do	Son	S	20		Engineman on Rail Engine		X			
					Desima do	Daur	S		16	Boot Maker					
					Martha do	Daur			13	Scholar					
					Ethel do	Daur			11	Scholar				Gloucestershire–Bristol	
					Walter do	Son		9		Scholar				do	
					Alfred do	Son		7						do	
					Clifford do	Son		3						do	
51			1		John P Mary Lodger	Lodger	Wid		52	Fish Hawker		X		Gloucestershire Bristol	
52	9 John St	1	10		John Lewis	Head	M	54		General Labourer		X		do	
53	1 North Place	1	2		Lavinia do	Wife	M		51	Charwoman		X		do	
					Ann Hall	Head	Wid		54	Fishwoman		X		do	
54	2 North Place	1	2		Thomas Abbott	Head	M	54		Painter		X		Dorset–Glastonbury	
					Mary J do	Wife	M		51					Gloucestershire–Bristol	
55	3 North Place	1	2		Ruth Smith	Head	Wid		69	Laundress		X		do – do	
					William J Louisa	Head	M		27	Mason Labourer		X		Somerset–Bath	
					Esther Kate do	Wife	M		40	Watercarrier				Gloucestershire–Bristol	
					James E do	Son		13		Scholar				do	
					William A do	Son		11		do				do	
					Mary A F do	Daur			6	do				do	
	Total of Houses and of Tenements with less than Five Rooms	5	1	7	Total of Males and Females...			14	16						

Note.—Draw the pen through such of the words of the headings as are inappropriate.

Fig. 4.1 *A page from the 1891 census for part of Bristol. Is this a working class or upper class area of the city? What sort of jobs did women do? How many "households" occupied 9 St John Street? How many rooms did the Horner Family occupy? Who else shared their home? (© Crown copyright)*

Discussion of the answers will raise a whole range of questions about life in the second half of the 19th century – the size of families, occupations, women's work and status in the family, popular names, rich and poor families, etc. Any of these can become starting points for further investigation using local evidence.

Focus on work: "How did people in this area earn a living in Victorian times?"

Start by providing a list of work categories such as Table 4.2, discussing it with the children so that they understand the main distinctions. KS3 children can be involved in drawing up the list. Simple broad categories are better than very detailed ones. There will always be some grey areas. In this kind of work with young children, the historical process, and the skills acquired through it, are sometimes more important than the absolute accuracy of the findings. The work then consists of looking at each entry in the "Rank, Profession or Occupation" column and recording the numbers who fall into each of the categories on the list. A number of the jobs will be unfamiliar to modern children, and part of the learning is to find out about these and to consider why they do not exist today.

Table 4.2 Categorising occupations

Professions	Doctor, Lawyer, Vicar, Teacher etc.
Factories and Businesses	Owners and Managers
	Foremen and skilled workers
	Clerks
	General workers and labourers
Shops, Hotels and Pubs	Shopkeepers, Innkeepers and Assistants
Farming	Farmers
	Skilled farm workers (shepherd, carter, etc.)
	Agricultural labourers
Independent Craftsmen	Blacksmith, wheelwright, etc.
Domestic Work	Housewives
	Domestic servants
	Other work at home
Not Needing to Work	Independent means
	Income from property, etc.
Not Able to Work	Retired
	Scholars
	Paupers
Others	Anything not covered by above

Children will now have a classified list of evidence which can be presented in the form of a pie chart or a bar chart to show graphically the numbers (or percentages) of workers in the different categories. A number of further inquiries can be made:

❐ What kind of work did the majority of people do?

❐ Is this work still common in the area today? Why?

❐ What sort of work did women do?

- ❐ What sort of work did boys and girls aged 12-16 do?
- ❐ What sort of people lived in your area in Victorian times? Were they mainly rich, poor or "middle class"?

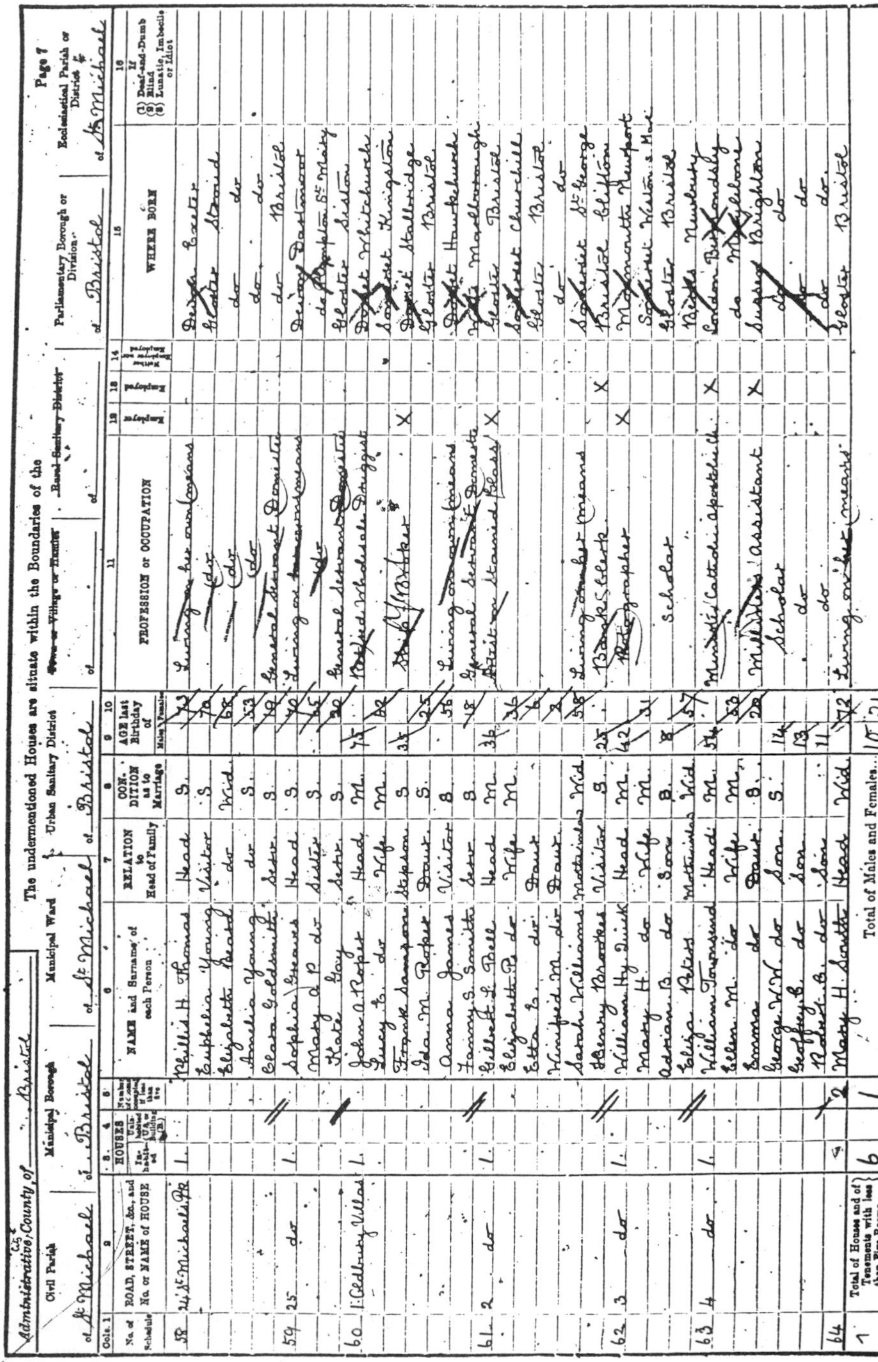

Administrative County of Bristol

The undermentioned Houses are situate within the Boundaries of the

Civil Parish of St Michael | Municipal Borough of Bristol | Municipal Ward of St Michael | Urban Sanitary District of Bristol | Town or Village or Hamlet of | Rural Sanitary District of | Parliamentary Borough or Division of Bristol | Ecclesiastical Parish or District of St Michael

Page 7

No. of Schedule	Road, Street, &c., and No. or Name of House	Houses: Inhabited	Houses: Uninhabited	Number of tenements occupied if less than five	Name and Surname of each Person	Relation to Head of Family	Condition as to Marriage	Age last Birthday: Males	Age last Birthday: Females	Profession or Occupation	Employer	Employed	Neither Employer nor Employed	Where Born	If (1) Deaf-and-Dumb (2) Blind (3) Lunatic, Imbecile or Idiot
58	24 St Michael's Pk	1			Phillis H. Thomas	Head	S.		73	Living on her own means				Devon Exeter	
					Euphelia Young	Visitor	S		70	do				Gloster Stroud	
					Elizabeth Beard	do	Wid.		68	do				do do	
					Amelia Young	do	S.		53	do				do do	
					Clara Goldsmith	Serv.	S.		19	General Servant Domestic				do Bristol	
59	25 do	1			Sophia Greaves	Head	S.		70	Living on own means				Devon Dartmoor	
					Mary A P do	Sister	S.		65	do				do Plympton St Mary	
					Kate Gay	Serv.	S.		20	General Servant Domestic				Gloster Siston	
60	1 Cedbury Villas	1			John A Roper	Head	M.	75		Retired Wholesale Druggist				Dorset Whitchurch	
					Lucy E. do	Wife	M.		62					Somerset Kingston	
					Frank Sampson	Stepson	S	35		Stock Broker	X			Dorset Stalbridge	
					Ida M. Roper	Daut.	S.		25					Gloster Bristol	
					Anna James	Visitor	S.		56	Living on own means				Dorset Hawkchurch	
					Fanny S. Smith	Serv.	S.		18	General Servant Domestic				Wilts Marlborough	
61	2 do	1			Gilbert L Bell	Head	M.	36		Artist in Stained Glass	X			Gloster Bristol	
					Elizabeth P. do	Wife	M.		36					Somerset Churchill	
					Etta E. do	Daut			6					Gloster Bristol	
					Winifred M. do	Daut.			2					do do	
					Sarah Williams	Mother-in-law	Wid		58	Living on her means				Somerset St George	
					Henry Brookes	Visitor	S.	25		Bank Clerk		X		Bristol Clifton	
62	3 do	1			William Hy. Quick	Head	M.	42		Photographer	X			Monmouth Newport	
					Mary H. do	Wife	M.		31					Somerset Weston s. Mare	
					Adrian B. do	Son	S.	8		Scholar				Gloster Bristol	
					Eliza Peters	Mother-in-law	Wid.		57					Berks Newbury	
63	4 do	1			William Townsend	Head	M.	54		Minister Catholic Apostolic Ch		X		London Bermondsey	
					Ellen M. do	Wife	M.		53					do Marylebone	
					Emma do	Daut.	S.		20	Milliner's assistant		X		Sussex Brighton	
					George W.W. do	Son	S.	14		Scholar				do do	
					Geoffrey E. do	Son		13		do				do do	
					Robert B. do	Son		11		do				do do	
64				2	Mary H. South	Head	Wid.		72	Living on her means				Gloster Bristol	
1	Total of Houses and of Tenements with less than Five Rooms	6		1	Total of Males and Females			10	21						

Note.—Draw the pen through such of the words of the headings as are inappropriate.

Fig. 4.2 A different part of Bristol. Compare the occupations and households with Figure 4.1 (© Crown copyright)

Comparing two different parts of a town, a wealthy area and a poor area

What sort of occupations are found in each area? What sort of houses did the people live in? Link the census with early OS maps and photographs and look at any surviving buildings. Which families kept servants? Were there any lodgers or boarders? Is there a difference in the size of households? Notice the column headed "Number of Rooms Occupied If Less Than Five" (1891). Look at the layout of streets, houses and gardens on the OS map. Can you work out how far people's homes were from the places where they worked? Discuss, write and draw about what it might have been like to live in the two areas.

Where did people come from?

Was the population of your study area mainly born and bred there? Using the "Where Born" column on the census make a distribution map showing where people not born locally came from. This can be done using 5, 10 and 20 mile radii, or plotting the number from each county on a map. Did all classes of people move about equally? Why did people move to your area? How did people travel?

The disadvantaged

Using the returns for your local union workhouse, look at the ages and circumstances of the inmates, including the final columns relating to physical and mental disability. Find the workhouse on a large scale map and look at its plan. This can be a starting point for finding out about the care of the poor and the elderly in Victorian Britain.

> IT

Manipulating data from census returns

Census returns are perhaps one of the best starting points for teachers wishing to use IT in the history curriculum. Transferring the information to a datafile is very straightforward: the information is already laid out in the table-like format common amongst data handling programs. However, there are a number of considerations to be made before teachers or pupils start transferring entries from the census returns to the computer.

Data handling programs vary in their ability to hold quantities of information and extract required information quickly. Therefore, it may be necessary to limit the number of entries to a reasonable amount, to ensure that information can be accessed quickly. At the same time you must ensure that there are enough entries to provide an accurate snapshot of the community, whilst providing an interesting range of individuals. For many data handling programs a datafile of about 600 people will be appropriate.

Teachers will also want to consider how best to organise the information from the census returns for entry into the computer. As historians we recognise the importance of preserving the historical accuracy of the original material. This includes repeating the various spelling errors, and other "mistakes" which inevitably occur in the originals. At the same time, the datafile will be used as a tool by the pupils to extend their understanding of life in the nineteenth century. The information must therefore be sensibly organised, to allow easy interrogation and analysis.

So it will be useful to include some additional information in the datafile which can be deduced or calculated from the original census returns. It may also be useful to provide some additional columns to hold some standardised spellings or abbreviations for county of birth, and a code or classification for occupational groupings, as described above.

It will also be necessary to make some compromises when creating datafiles from census returns. Enumerators seldom repeated information: census returns are littered with "do" or "ditto". However, a datafile containing dozens of families with the surname "ditto" is not very helpful. Therefore it will be necessary to enter the relevant information rather than entering "ditto" whenever it occurs.

When defining the fieldnames for a datafile of census returns, the suggestions in Table 4.3 may be helpful. Depending on your data handling program, it may be necessary to abbreviate some of the fieldnames and/or to restrict the number of fields.

Table 4.3 Field names for census analysis

Schedule Number	Almost certainly in sequence, but not necessarily starting at 'one'.
Address	The name or address of the house
Forename and Surname	These are stored together in one column on original census returns. However, it makes sense to store them in separate fields in the datafile, so that children can search for individuals by their surname
Relationship to Head	It will be necessary to agree, before creating the datafile, what common abbreviations or spellings to use for Relationship, so that children can search the datafile easily using the agreed abbreviations
Marital condition	Again, this is best coded (so that, for example, "Wi", "Wid" and Widow" appear in the same way)
Sex	On original census returns, age is entered in two columns. For your database, create one column headed 'Sex', so children can examine the different roles of men and women in the 19th century
Age	This should consist of numbers only, so the data handling program can produce sensible charts or graphs of the information. Children less than one year old should be entered as "0". So, a child of nine months in the census is not entered as such (nor as "0.75"). Exact ages can be entered in the Remarks column
Occupation	Longer entries can be continued in the Remarks column
Town of Birth/ County of Birth	If two fields are made from the entry in the 'Where born' census column, a greater variety of searches can be made by pupils
Remarks	Entries for "deaf", "dumb", etc, as well as the exact age of infants, and any extra information from the Occupation field are placed here.

Additional information can easily be calculated from the original census returns, which can assist children when they are interrogating the census datafile. Some examples might be as in Table 4.4.

Table 4.4 Calculations from census data

Household Size

Family Size	This can be calculated from the Relationship to Head column, and clear guidance will be needed from the teacher to those entering the data to ensure consistency throughout the datafile as to what constitutes a familial relationship.
Occupational Code	Many times one wants children to examine all those involved in a particular type of occupation. We know that an Agricultural Labourer is the same as an "Ag lab", and that this occupation is similar to a Farmer or Shepherd. But the computer does not possess this understanding. A coding system can therefore be used, which groups similar occupations together (see the section above "Focus on work", and this can assist pupils in this sort of investigation. A more comprehensive coding system, derived from enumerators' books, can be found in *Nineteenth Century Society* (ed. E.A. Wrigley), CUP, 1972.
County Code	A standard three-letter code for the "County of Birth" will enable pupils to find all the individuals born in specific counties, regardless of the variety of spellings employed in the County of Birth (census) column. Using both Occupations Code and County Code, children can ask the computer to search these columns (and therefore find individuals which match more easily), and then to print or display the information from the Occupations and County of Birth columns to provide original spellings etc.
Country	If the census returns for your community detail certain individuals born abroad it may be useful to include a field to hold this information.

If teachers are using the 1891 census returns there are two additional fields which may be useful, the information for which first appeared on this census.

Rooms	This would contain the number of rooms occupied, if fewer than five. (However, since this information is entered only for those households to which it applies, it may not be very helpful).
Employment	This would contain the details as to whether the person was an employer, employed or neither.

Once a datafile of census returns has been prepared, pupils can use the computer to investigate and analyse this historical evidence in a variety of ways, and to reach conclusions based on their examination of the evidence. Pupils using data handling programs can progress from individual enquiries to generalisations. They can form and test hypotheses, thus engaging in historical research. In addition, many data handling programs allow children to produce graphs, charts and tables of information. Moreover, children can quickly and easily experiment with the method of displaying the information, which can greatly assist their interpretation of the evidence (for example, see Figure 4.3).

Creating a datafile of census returns can be a time-consuming exercise, but one which can be of great value. It may be sensible to view such an activity as a long term project, to be carried out over a number of terms with different children participating. Teachers may also find that local census returns have already been transcribed and keyed into a datafile. Contact your local secondary school or local history society to see if they know of material suitable for your use.

Fig. 4.3 A typical IT output

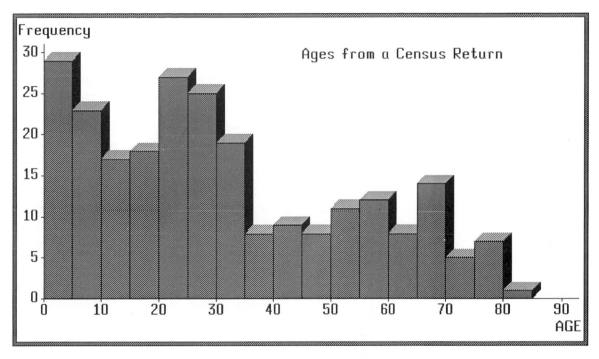

PROBLEMS

Possible difficulties using censuses
Handwriting

This may look difficult to children at first but should not really be a problem after a little practice. (One imaginative strategy is to do a session on copperplate writing and let children try to write in this style themselves so that they become more familiar with it.) If it really is difficult, try using A3 size copies or as a last resort transcribe the entries and let children work from a typescript. (See also the suggestions for computer based work.) Even if using a transcript or computer database the pupils should also see some originals, because this is part of the excitement of history. In general it is best to select examples which are reasonably easy to read.

Abbreviations

Children will have to become familiar with the standard abbreviations used by the enumerators, especially "do." for "ditto".

Deletions

Often the entries look as though they have been crossed out but this is simply because they have been "ticked" by drawing a line through them when statistics were being extracted.

5 Commercial directories

What are directories?

The first commercial directory was produced in London in 1677, and they have continued to be published up to the present day, (*Thompson's* and *Yellow Pages* are the modern equivalents). They particularly flourished in the nineteenth and early twentieth centuries and large numbers have survived. Some were published by the Post Office but a number of other firms also produced them. Kelly, perhaps the best known producer of directories, was criticized in Parliament for abusing his official position as Inspector of Letter carriers for the Post Office to collect information for the directories he published privately. Firms like Pigot & Co. employed many agents to undertake the difficult task of collecting information all over the country and keeping it up to date.

The main purpose of directories was to provide local business information in the form of lists of names. Information for a large city or town would occupy a whole volume, while smaller towns and villages would be included in county volumes, where entries might vary from a dozen lines to several pages. The range of information included was the decision of individual publishers, but a more or less standard format was eventually adopted. Directories for large towns were revised and published annually from the late 19th century, but county volumes came out at longer intervals. In spite of attempts to revise the contents regularly, the information was sometimes out of date, and was often incomplete in that not all tradespeople were included.

There are usually three kinds of information in directories:

❑ General information about the place, its history, church, schools, postal service, carriers, coaches, etc.

❑ Lists of inhabitants. For villages in a county directory, this will only include the wealthier and more important residents. In town directories there may be fuller alphabetical lists as well as a street by street list. All of these will show heads of households only.

❑ The main list of tradespeople. Again this may be a short alphabetical list for a village, or a full classified list for a large town.

In addition to the text there were usually several pages of advertisements.

Apart from the general commercial directories dealt with in this chapter, there were specialised directories of particular trades and professions. These are less likely to be useful in KS2 history.

and the principal landowner. The soil is clay; subsoil, blue clay and chalk-stones. The chief crops are wheat, barley, oats, peas and beans. In 1861 the population was 708; the area is 3,386 acres. The soil is strong, stiff, and cold.

WEST END is a mile south from the village; Hill Farm, a mile west; Up End, about a mile west; North End is a mile and a quarter north-west; Bury End is a mile and a quarter north-east.

Parish Clerk, Reuben Odell.

POST OFFICE.—George Davy, receiver. Letters received through Bedford at 7.15 p.m.; dispatched at 5.20 a.m. Bedford is the nearest money order office

Free School, George Davy, master; Mrs. Mary Davy, mistress

CARRIERS TO & FROM BEDFORD.—James Mapley, monday, wednesday & saturday; Wallinger, wednesday & saturday; George Glidewell passes through to Bedford from North Crawley, on wednesday & saturday

Brodrick Hon. & Rev. Alan, M.A. [vicar], Vicarage
Barker John Berrill, farmer, Bury farm
Bass Mary Ann & Son, farmers
Bass Charles, farmer
Bazley Charles, wheelwright
Bonney John, *White Horse*
Fensom (Mrs.), farmer, North End farm
Henman James, farmer, West End
Henman Philip Hart, farmer, Wick End farm

Landon William, farmer, Up End
Lay Alfred, baker
Lay John, shoe maker
Leaberry John, farmer, West End
Leaberry William, farmer, Hill farm
Odell Jacob, farmer
Odell William, shopkpr. & pork butcher
Pettit James, farmer, West End
Pheasey Amos, farmer, Dropshort
Slater Abel, *Dog & Duck*, & shopkeeper & pork butcher

Summerlin Austin, *Royal George*, & blacksmith
Walker Lewis, farmer, West End
Walker Wm. & Wm. Bartram, farmers
Warwick Richard, tinman
White Jonathan, tailor
White Thomas, shoe maker
Whitmee Thomas, farmer
Wood Joseph, farmer, West End
Wood Susan (Mrs.), farmer, West End

STANBRIDGE is a hamlet and ecclesiastical parish, in the civil parish of Leighton Buzzard, 3 miles east-by-south from Leighton Buzzard, and about 4 north-west from Dunstable, in the hundred of Manshead, union of Leighton Buzzard, county court district of Leighton Buzzard, rural deanery of Dunstable, archdeaconry of Bedford, and diocese of Ely. The church of St. John the Baptist has a square embattled tower with 5 bells: the chancel is Perpendicular English, aisles the same: the nave has four bays, the arches on the north side being loftier than those on the south. The living is a vicarage, yearly value £100, in the gift of the vicar of Leighton Buzzard, and held by the Rev. Gregory Edward Whyley, M.A., of Trinity College, Cambridge.

Here are three Sunday schools and two Wesleyan chapels. The straw plait business gives occupation to a great many persons. Major W. E. Hanmer is lord of the manor. The principal landowners are Col. Gilpin, Mr. Lawford, Mr. Twidell and Mr. Brown. The soil is of a kind of clay; subsoil, clay. The chief crops are wheat, barley, beans and peas. The population in 1861 was 554; the area is 1,400 acres.

Parish Clerk, Thomas Eames.

Letters through Leighton Buzzard, arrive at 8.15 a.m.; dispatched at 6 p.m. Leighton Buzzard is the nearest money order office

Burridge John, farmer
Eames Joseph, *Five Bells*
Eames Thomas, farmer
Ellingham John, beer retailer
Flemon Benjamin, farmer
Flint John, boot & shoe maker
Franklin Andrews, farmer
Franklin John, farmer

Gadsden Thomas, farmer
George Frederick, beer retailer
Goodman Jesse, straw plait dealer
Gurney George, farmer
Hawkins George, farmer
Horn William, boot & shoe maker
Jones George, farmer
Labrun Joseph, baker

Olney George, butcher & beer retailer
Olney John, farmer
Scott Joseph, tailor
Tims David, wheelwright
Tims Samuel, plait dealer
Twidell John, farmer
Wilks Josiah, farmer & plait dealer
Wilks Josiah, shopkeeper

LITTLE STAUGHTON (or STAUGHTON PARVA) is a picturesque parish and village, situated on an eminence, 10 miles north from Bedford, 6 north-west from St. Neots, and 5 south from Kimbolton, on the borders of the county, in the hundred of Stodden, union and county court district of St. Neots, rural deanery of Eaton, archdeaconry of Bedford, and diocese of Ely. The church of All Saints is a very neat structure, consisting of chancel and spire of freestone: its architecture is Perpendicular Gothic: it contains an ancient shrine tomb. The register dates from the year 1598. The living is a rectory, yearly value £278, with residence, in the gift of Corpus Christi College, Oxford, and held by the Rev. Francis Robinson, M.A., of that college, who resides at Stonesfield, Woodstock, Oxfordshire. Here is a National school, at which about 500 children attend.

There is a large chapel belonging to the Baptists, affording accommodation to 700 persons, with a burying-ground attached: the attendance of children at the Baptist Sunday school averages 180, chiefly non-parishioners. The lords of the manor are the representatives of the late Francis Pym, Esq. The soil is heavy; subsoil, clay. The chief crops are wheat, barley and oats. The population in 1861 was 572; the area is about 1,660 acres.

Parish Clerk, John Manfell.

Letters through St. Neots arrive at 8 a.m.; dispatched at 5.30 p.m. Kimbolton is the nearest money order office

National School, John Mantell, master

CARRIER.—Mrs. Susan Saunders, to St. Neots, every thursday; to Bedford, every saturday

Parish Mr. Joseph
Robinson Rev. Thomas [Baptist]
Wilkins Rev. John Theophilus, B.A. curate

COMMERCIAL.

Allen Josiah, farmer
Barleyman Joseph, shopkeeper
Bellamy Edward, wheelwright
Brightman Shadrach, farmer

Ekins Christopher, farmer
Ekins Joseph, farmer
Flanders Robert, *Shoulder of Mutton*
Gray William, shopkeeper
Hawkins James, beer retailer
Hawkins William, *Kangaroo*
Jarvis John, shopkeeper
Matthews James, blacksmith
Minney Henry, farmer

Minney John, beer retailer
Minney Spencer, *Crown*
Palmer Samuel, cowkeeper
Peacock Silas, blacksmith
Pestell James, farmer
Rawlings Joseph, harness maker
Reynolds Samuel, farmer
Savage Titus, tailor
Sisman William, shoe maker & farmer

STEPPINGLEY is a village and parish, 2½ miles south-west from Ampthill, and 10 south from Bedford, in the hundred of Redbornestoke, union and county court district of Ampthill, rural deanery of Fleete, archdeaconry of Bedford, and diocese of Ely, bounded on the north-east by the Flitt, a tributary of the Ouse. The church of St. Bartholomew was rebuilt in 1860, by the Duke of Bedford and the then rector, of the sandstone quarried on the estate: it is in the Early Decorated and Perpendicular styles, with a tower containing 4 bells, nave, north aisle, and chancel, and it is seated with open oak benches and paved with encaustic tiles. The register dates from the year 1647. The living is a rectory, yearly value about £260, with residence, in the gift

of the Lord Chancellor, and held by the Rev. Edward James Paget, M.A., of St. John's College, Oxford. There is a National school, and a small Wesleyan chapel. The Duke of Bedford is lord of the manor and the principal landowner. The soil is chiefly sand; subsoil, sand. The chief crops are wheat, barley, clover, and turnips. The population in 1861 was 365; the area is 1,218 acres.

Parish Clerk, Thomas Hollis.

Letters received through Ampthill arrive at 10 a.m.; dispatched at 4.30 p.m. Ampthill is the nearest money order office

National School, Miss Vern, mistress

Cook Hannah (Mrs.), farmer, Towns-end farm
Farmar William, wheelwright
Furze Jane (Mrs.), farmr. Steppingley pk

Gregory Thomas, baker
Lee John, beer retailer
Lee William, farm bailiff to S. Seabrook, esq. Frog hall

Marriott William, farmer, Warren farm
Monk Mary (Mrs.), beer retailer
Phillips Ann (Mrs.), *French Horn*
Phillips Thomas, butcher & shopkeeper

Fig. 5.1 A typical page from a county directory (Post Office, 1869)

WHERE?

Where to find directories

HSUs

Commercial directories and the National Curriculum

Local commercial directories from the 19th and 20th centuries (and perhaps some even earlier 18th century examples) will be found in local history libraries and record offices throughout the country. They are often on open shelves and although they are rather fat and heavy volumes, extracts can usually be photocopied.

At KS2, directories can be used to provide local evidence to support the SUs *Victorian Britain* and *Britain Since 1930,* and as part of the SU on Local History. They can contribute to a long term study of transport (because they include details of local communications).

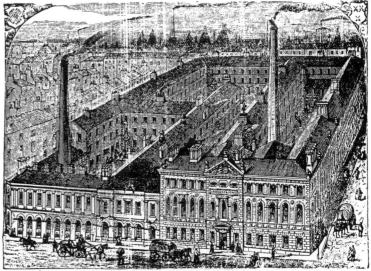

Fig. 5.2 Advertisement from a Kelly's directory, 1882

At KS3, they are relevant to SU3 *Britain 1750-c1900*, where they can be used to give a local dimension to commercial and industrial topics looking at the impact of the Industrial Revolution on the local area. Transport and communications can be illustrated as well as local businesses.

Using commercial directories

Being printed documents and consisting largely of lists, directories present few reading problems for children. The amount of information in a town volume would be overwhelming and, as with the census, it is sensible to concentrate on a small area – perhaps a street or the area around the school. When studying the Victorian period it is possible to use Directories alongside census

TRADES DIRECTORY.   LAU 653

BLANCHE'S HAND LAUNDRY

The Largest and Best Equipped Hand Laundry in NORTH OXFORD

No Machinery   **Hand Work only**

ESTABLISHED *over 30 Years*

—*Collection and Delivery*—

ISLIP ROAD, SUNNYMEAD, OXFORD

TELEPHONE : SUMMERTOWN 58035
PLEASE QUOTE THIS ADVERTISEMENT

LAUNDRIES.

Axtell Mrs. Thos. Woodstock rd. Yarnton
BLANCHE'S HAND LAUNDRY, 91 Islip road, Sunnymead. Telephone Number 58035. See advertisement

Busby Mrs. Alice, 11 Grove st. Summertown
Bushnell Miss H. 13 Elm's rd. H
CITY LAUNDRY (THE) (Bennetts Ltd. dyers & cleaners, proprietors), Abbey place, St. Ebbe's. Tel. 2493

Electric Laundry (Oxford) Ltd. 6 Harpes road, Summertown
Faulkner Mrs. Edith H. 77 Plantation rd
Faulkner F. W., Bagley wood, Kennington

FRENCH LAUNDRY SUNNY-MEADE LTD. (THE), 44, 46 & 48 Islip road (Telephone No. Summertown 5517) ; reg. office, 15 Magdalen st
Haynes Jsph. 71 Crescent rd. C
Heard Mrs. W. 25 Church st. H
Horwood Mrs. Sarah E. 3 Elm's rd. H

HYGIENIC LAUNDRY (ABING-DON) LTD. (THE) (expert shirt & collar dressers for high-class family work), Caldecott road ; receiving offices, 20A. Lombard street, Abingdon (Tel. Abingdon 269) & High street, New H
Kerry Chas. 33 High st. Headington Quarry
Kimber Mrs. H. Horspath
Lee Ching Sing, 60 Cowley road
Luckett Miss Emma, 78 Harpes rd. Summertown
OXFORD SANITARY STEAM LAUNDRY CO. LTD. (S. T. Glass-poole, manager), Littlemore. Tel. Cowley 7050
Star Imperial Laundry, 201 Banbury rd.; receiving offices, 135 Cowley rd. & 32 Walton st
SWAN LAUNDRY, WITNEY (" Float-ironed" & "Fully Finished" services ; dry cleaning). Phone 98 & our van will call

Fig. 5.3 Classified trades list from Kelly's Directory of Oxford, 1934

returns, but one of their great advantages is that they are available for the period after 1891 when the census is not. Thus they are a particularly useful source for any study with a focus on trades, shops or occupations in the *Britain Since 1930* SU. Even when the census is available directories are a particularly easy source of information about occupations because they contain classified lists.

Finding out about local trades and craftsmen

If the study area is a village or small town pupils can use directories to find out what trades and crafts were present in the past and this will inevitably provoke comparisons with the present day. Such a study is likely to provide striking evidence of change, in that the variety of trades in small communities in the past will almost certainly have disappeared today. Some trades present in Victorian times may be unfamiliar to pupils and they can go on to find out about the nature of the work and the products, using a dictionary or perhaps the recently reprinted *Book of Trades or Library of Useful Arts* published in 1811. It is also a good idea to look at the actual products in museums or at least to find pictures in books. Advertisements in the directories can provide additional information, perhaps including prices.

Looking at shops in a town

Use a town directory to find out what sort of shops existed in the main shopping street in Victorian times or since 1930. Change and continuity can be observed if several directories of different dates are used, and, as always, questions asked about why these changes have happened. Other sources should also be used to find out more about shops, such as large-scale old maps to plot their position in the street (and it may be possible to identify the site or even the building today), old photographs, advertisements in the directory itself or in old newspapers, and the Census up to 1891. Oral history could also be used to provide memories of shops in the 1930s or 1940s. When making comparisons with today the modern shopping centre plans produced for many towns by C. Goad Ltd. can be very useful.

Focus on transport and communications

Many directories include information about postal services (times of delivery and collection) and, in the 19th century, details of long distance coaches and local carriers' carts. This kind of information is difficult to find anywhere else. Children can use it as part of a general study of land transport or to investigate particular topics such as the effects of the railways on road transport, to look in detail at travel by coach or the local service provided by the carriers. On a map of the area, places served by carriers or coaches can be plotted and charts made of distances and frequency of journeys.

Illustrating an aspect of domestic life

Kelly's Directory of Oxford for 1934 (Figure 5.3) shows a large number of laundries in the district (notice a Chinese and a French laundry). At this date it was harder to find servants, and domestic washing machines were still rare, so better off households sent

110 IFF

OXFORD

IFFLEY ROAD—continued.
276 Orme Miss
278 Morley Mrs
280 Madden Miss
282 Ross Hubert Edwd
284 Brown Miss Catherine
286 Pether Mrs. F
.... here is Fairacres rd.....
288 Boreham Fredk. G
290 Weber Jn
292 Bayliss Wm. Jn. S
294 Thomas Richard P
296 Hiles Herbt. Clarence
... here is Addison cres ...
298 Harrison Arthur John
300 Nutter Tom
302 James George Edward
304 Hector Edgar Geo
Walker Fredk. Arth.
(2 Donnington lodge)
Page Ernest (1 Don-
nington lodge)
.. here is Donnington la ...
EarlAlbertJohn,private
hotel (Freelands)
... here is Radcliffe rd ...
350 Byford Francis Philip
352 Smith Alfred Charles
... here is Freelands rd ...
354 Pickett Fredk
356 Gardner Bert
358 Thompson Arth. H
360 Wilkes Harold
362 Longhurst William
364 Heaton Leonard B
366 Adams Fredk
368 Vine John
Dyer Frank, confectnr
City MotorCo.(Oxford)
Ltd
South Midland Motor
Services Ltd. (garage)

IFFLEY TURN (Iffley),
from Carell road.
.... here is Carell rd ......
Butler Russell (The Cross-
ways)
West Rd. decrtr. (works)
Lansdell & Son, coal mers
Forrest Lady (Iffley Turn
ho)
DraperFrankJ.(Ellesmere)
GibbsPercyA.(Southwaye)
Blay Mrs. (Gursedune)
JoelWm.J.(TheBungalow)

Spokes Jn. N. (The Rise)
Jessup Wm. (Fair view)
Graham Eric Chas. (Braye
cott)
Macpherson Mrs. (town
Len)
Young Miss (Meade)
Blanchett Arth. Rd. (Bel-
stone)
Walklett Mrs. E. A. (Oak-
dene)

Iffley Turn cottages.
See Church way, Iffley.

ISISSTREET(St.Aldate's),
from 44 St. Aldate's st.
SOUTH SIDE.
1 Benwell Miss
2 Benwell Miss Muriel C
3 Millin Walter Henry
4 Harris Joseph
5 Elmer Miss
6 Haines Mrs. C. E
7 ChandlerLemuel Joseph
8 Hitchman Percival
Bernard
8A, Ashbourne Mrs. S
8B, Bartlett Fred
COLLAR FRANK,
AND scull maker oar
9 Miller Hy. Jn
Oxford Corporation
Wharf
NORTH SIDE.
10 Green Wm. Thos
11 Smith Ernest
12 Williams Robert
13 Sloper Sidney Arth
14 Butterfield Fras
15 Ward Harry
17 Harvey Mrs
18 Shirley Fredk. Geo
19 Biddle Misses
20 Hounslow Mrs

ISLIP ROAD (Summer-
town),from 15 Hernes road
to 27 Water Eaton road.
NORTH SIDE.
1 Walker Alfred James
3 Prickett Miss Alice,
dressma
7 Somerton Fredk. Jn

9 Johnson Giles
17 Thompson Wm. Guy
Duncan
19 Jones Norman Fredk. V
21 Sammons Miss
23 Dixon & Son, carriers
23 Dixon Fredk. Harold
27 Edmonds Wltr. & Son,
dairymen
27 Edmonds Cyril Wltr
29 Hickman Arth. L
31 Neale Joseph Abraham,
boot maker
33 Biavois Victor
35 Whitlock Edwin
37 Blackwell Frederick
39 Biggs Wm. Edwd
41 Gee James
43 Evans Mrs
45 Gardner Jsph
47 Loveridge Walter
49 Powell Joseph Patrick
51 Dawson George William
53 Stone John
55 Nash Wm. Edgar L
57 Hunt Regnld
59 Inness Mrs
61 Nash Mrs
63 Bowerman Rd
63A, Clinkard Rd. Hum-
phry, shopkpr
65 Clinch Colin Harold
67 Soper Arthur Leonard
69 Inswell Stanley
71 Bowerman Harold Hy
73 Dedman Thos
75 Stone John William
77 Pitts Albert, watch ma
79 Bryan Percival James
81 Hathaway Wm. Hy
83 Cooke Jas
85 Jones Mrs
87 Lloyd Jsph
89 SlaughterFrederickWm
91 BLANCHE'S HAND
LAUNDRY (Mrs. F. B.
Layer, proprietress),
Telephone Number
58035. See advert
SOUTH SIDE.
2 Kuibbs Mrs
2 Simmonds Miss
4 Woodbridge Mrs
6 Nicholls Thomas Wm
8 Williamson Capt. Herbt.
Charles

STREET DIRECTORY.

JAM 111

JACKSTRAWS LANE
(Headington Hill), from
Marston road to Pullens
hue.
Brown Wm. C. (Sunnyside)
Matthews Geo. H. (Way-
side)
Field Lewis, farmer (Plow-
man's farm)
Seaward Harry (Noyon)
Keen Col. Fredk. Stewart,
C.B.,D.S.O. (Rushwood)
Armour Alfd. Edwd. M.A.
(Overmead)
Thorpe Jn. E.(Underwood)
Price Hy. Habberley, sen.
(Hillside)
Price Hy. Habberley, jun.
M.A.,B.Sc. (fellow & Uni-
versity lecturer in Phil-
osophy, Trinity college)
(Hillside)
Forster Arnold J. M.B.E.,
M.A.(fellow&estates bur-
sar, Magdalen college)
(St. Mary's)
Houghton Rev. Canon
Edwd. Jn Walford D.D.
(St. Michael's)
Williams Sir Jn. Fischer
C.B.E., K.C. (Bowling
Green ho)
Low Lt.-Col. Chas. F. G.
(Little Orchard)
Smith Hy. A. J.P. (Field
ho)
Blackman Wm. (Cowley
House lodge)

10 Berry Cyril Joseph
12 Cumming Maurice L.
14 Ludlow Mrs
16 Simpson George B
18 Clay Thomas
20 Reed Miss
22 Hatton Ernest R
24 Inness Geo. Rd
28 Edgington Wm. Arth
30 Hiles Mrs. Lydia
32 Fleetwood Henry
34 Honey Wm. Kenwood
40 Morris William
42 Robinson Ernest William
44, 46 & 48 THE FRENCH
LAUNDRY SUNNY-
MEADE LIMITED.
Tel. No. Summer-
town 5517
50 Smith George
52 Leverett Alfred
54 Edney Rt. Hy
56 Locke Miss
58 Norgrove Miss
60 Green Henry
62 Gibbard William
64 Hastings Mrs
66 Barrett Miss
68 Blake Arth. Geo
70 Hedges Robert Harry
72 Horn Arth. Granville
74 Collins Joseph
76 Silk Albt. Wm
78 Codd Mrs
80 Honey William
82 Honey Regnld. W
84 Hopcraft Abram John
86 Brockless Miss E. A
88 Wood Hy
90 Hedges Alfd. E. shpkpr
92 Prickett William
96 Fleetwood William
98 Morris Charles Ernest
100 Malvern Walter
102 Waldron Henry George

JACK DAW LANE, from
Iffley road.
.... here is Stratford st ....
.... here is Ferry la......
Cox Jsph. smallholder
Cox Wilfred Thos.chimney
cleaner

3 Ivings John
4 Pulker Edward William
5 Allum John, boot maker
6 Gardiner Miss
7 Macready James
8 Smith Charles
11 Childe Miss
12 Lord Arth
13 Lord Frank
14 Thornton Benj
15 Leonard HaroldWilliam
16 Chapman Thos. Fredk
17 Phelps Wm. Geo
18 Veale Frederick Thomas
19 Beckley Percival
20 Betnay Chas. Cammack
21 Green Mrs. Emma
22 Heath Geo. Osborne,
cabnt. mkr
23 Sastry Mrs
24 Hitchman Mrs
25 Trinder David Wm
26 Evans Isaac O
27 Barrett Enos
28 Francis Charles
29 Peters Mrs
30 CoombesWilliam Henry
31 Hine Mrs
32 Holloway Mrs
33 Bartlett Ernest Hy
38 Tanner Wm. boot maker
39 & 39A, Standbrook J.C.
& Sons, shopkprs
40 Reeve William Thomas
41 Grant Mrs
42 Mundy George Edwin
43 Redhead Herbert
44 Besson Harry
45 Millin Wm. tailor
46 Bryant Jas. C
NORTH-WEST SIDE.
..... here is Cowley rd......
47 & 48 Bull Frank M.
beer retlr
49 Wakelin Mrs
50 Ball Mrs
51 Timms Chas. Wm
52 Deadman Herbert Geo
53 Haynes Miss
54 Scarsbrook Miss Elsie,
teacher of music
55 Harris Arth. C
..... here is St. Mary's rd. ...
56 Hill Mrs
57 Wilmot Jn. Arth
58 Allaway Frederick

JAMESPL. (St. Clement's),
from 23 Caroline street.
1 Young Francis
2 Day Mrs. Dorothy M.
shopkpr
2 Day Hy. Jas. Thos
3 Collier Mrs
4 Cardy Mrs
5 Ramsden Jn
6 Chesterman Wm. Richd

JAMES ST. (Cowley St.
John), from 119 Iffley road
to 136 Cowley road.
SOUTH-EAST SIDE.
1 Salmon Charles Andrew
2 Everest Miss

Fig. 5.4 Street directory from Kelly's Directory of Oxford, 1934

OXFORD STREET DIRECTORY—1894-5.

163   IFF

29 Brightwell&Co.bill pstrs
30 Howe Brothers, tailors
31 Hedges & Son, tailors
32 Cummings Mrs
33 Piper Matthew G. H
34 Jones James
35 HineJn.Andrew,carpenter, joiner,undertkr.&c
36 Allen William, mineral water maker
37 Homœopathic Dispensary (John McLachlan M.D., F.R.C.S., B.Sc. medical supt)
38 Butler Edmund
38 St. John's Ambulance Station
39 & 40 Rowley Mrs
41 Heritage Edward
42 Turner Henry
.....here is Fisher row (Upper)
EAST SIDE.
Iffley road, from The Plain, St. Clement's.
1 Cape of Good Hope P.H. Walter Burgess
1 Osborne Alfred
3 Hounslow Chas. painter
5 Kerby William Henry, university lodgings
7 Douglas Robert Langton
9 Malpas Richard
11 MoonWilliam,university bedel
13 Moody James
15 Moody Edwin
17 Ridley Mrs. (Ivy Dene)
19 Beesley Chas. university lodgings
21 Beesley Harry,
23 Hazeldine Rev. Frdk. John [curate of St. Clement's]
25 Higgins Joseph Thomas
27 Wheeler Isaac
29 Shribb Mrs
31 Packford A.photographr
31 Packford Mrs. lodg. ho

OXF.

33 Gawn William
35 Howard Mrs
35 Cooke Nathaniel, insurance agent
41 Chapman Mrs. Ana, lodging house
43 Cricketers' Arms, Harry Read
.....here is Circus st
45 Alden William Hayes
47 Jeffery Alfred, pianoforte agent (The Isis)
47 & 149Griffin Edwd.grcr
47 Jeffery Mrs. Alfred, boarding ho. (The Isis)
49 Knott Frederick John
53 Plumridge Hy. MUS.DOC
55 Stemson Miss
57 Fisher Richard
59 Brooks Robert
61 Crump George
.....here is Temple st
65 Neale Miss Georgina, lodging house
67 Cox Miss
69 TurrellWalterJohn M.D. physician & surgeon
75 Carter Mrs
.....here is Stockmore st
77 Hemming Miss
79 Gough Charles
81 Johnson Arthur
83 Burley Henry, lodg. ho
85 Newton Rev.Isaac[Wes]
87 Richardson Miss Laura, boarding house
89 Baker Mrs
89 Baker Miss Elizabeth A.
91 Beak Mrs
93 Hugo Mrs
95 Mawer John William
97 Watts William
99 Brabant Charles
101 Owen William
101 Castle John C
PILLAR LETTER BOX
.....here is Marston st
103 Griffiths James Francis
105 Tocqua Mrs
107 Crawley Miss
109 Savage William
111 Dodson Mrs
113 Higgs Rev.Edwd.Hood
115 Grimbly Mrs. James
117 Latimer Mrs
.....here is James st

121 Beckley Charles Henry
127 Hughes Nicholas
131 Surman Thomas
133 Humphreys William C, undertaker
135 Wyatt J.
137 Hooper Thomas
139 Tidmarsh Thomas
141 Rogers John
143 Lediard Mrs
145 Page William
147 & 149Griffin Edwd.grcr
151 Archer Thomas
153 Harris Mrs
155 Clifford David Price
157 Sankey Mrs
161 Roberts Rev. Wilson Aylesbury M.A
163 Boulter Wm. beer retlr
.....here is Bullingdon rd
165 DodtlsTomWm.MUS.DOC
167 Sheard James
169 Archer Charles
171 Faber Mrs
173 Alden Edward C
175 Fish Benjamin
177 Hore Mrs
179 Kent Mrs
181 Francombe Samson
183 Gmelin Rev. Frdk
187 Macphail Rev.Edmund W. St. Maur M.A
.....here is Henley st
189 Lane John Robert
193 Hartland Thomas (Geo. B.A.Lond. school
195 Martin Rev.Herbert Jn
199 Butler George Cooper
201 Cotes Mrs
203 Clarke Eaton
205 Walker W. H
207 Busher Edmund
211 Fowler Mrs
213 Knapp Rev.Hy.Jn.M.A
215 Tidmarsh Cornelius
.....here is Aston st
217 Dodwell A.H.(Gustandael)
219 King James Francis
221 Rowton Rev.Rupert.Jas
223 Mallam George B. physician & surgeon
235 Dormor James Mace (Melcombe)
.....here is Stanley rd
237 BomfordJas.(Woodvw)

ISI

IFFLEY ROAD—continued.
239 St. Basil's Home for Aged Women
.....here is Chester st
241 Thomas Rbt.M.A.school (Danemead)
WALL LETTER BOX
243 Newport.John, beer ret
.....here is Magdalen rd
247 Clark Alfred
251 Steel John
253 Annetts George
255 Weippert Mrs
257 Davies Mrs. Howell
259 Gibbs Miss, ladies' schl
261 Margetts Frdk.Arthur
263 Cross William Frdk. (Chiswell house)
.....here is Percy st
265 Hazard Henry
265 Burborough Robert,cab proprietor
267 Dunn Mrs
269 Miller Mrs
271 Walton Charles, florist
273 Hodgson Samuel
275 Oakley Francis
277 Jacobs Mrs. Adelaide, laundress
279 Benson Charles
.....here is Charles st
291 Tims Mrs
293 Kemshead Chaloner LL.B.Lond
.....here is Howard st
297 Townsend Mrs
299 Shirley Mrs.shopkeeper (Mileway cottage)
WEST SIDE.
Sherwood Rev. William Edward M.A. (head master of Magdalen College school)
Christ Church Cricket Ground
ArmstrongEdward(Redho) Oxford University Athletic Ground,
C. N. Jackson, treas
Dorrill CharlesChristopher, (Rustdene)
Maunsell Staff-Commander William Hare R.N. (The Moorings)
Bacon John (Dalkeith)
Spokes George Newcomb (Cranham)
Cooper George Hy. (Incot)

ISI   OXFORD STREET DIRECTORY—1894-5.   164

Gould James (Rouslon)
Butler Alexander E. H. (Danemead)
CooperThos.(Spring valley)
Maltby John Chadwick (Heatherfield)
GreatbatchArth.(May bnk)
Baker Harry (Riversdale)
Elford Mrs. (Pensilva)
Nicholas T. (San Grabiel)
Smith Thackwell (Pitville)
Thompson William, steward to Littlemore Asylum (Maizena)
de Salis Randolph (Fairacres)
Winter Alfred, accountant (Skirbeck)
Meadows Geo. D.(Lucerne)
.....here is Fairacres rd
Venables Sydney (Donnington lodge)
.....here is New Iffley
Parker Mrs. (Freelands)

Isis street (St. Aldate's), from 44 St. Aldate's st.
1 & 2 Boswell Thomas Girdler, coal merchant
3 Smith Mrs. Frank, lodging house
3 Thomas Rev. W. Henry Griffith A.K.C.L
4 Eyles Charles
8 Elmer Thomas Henry
8 Gillams William
9 Tims Thos. boat builder
9 Crane Henry James
Oxford Corporation City Water Works Storage Yard
Oxford Corporation Whf. (W. H. White, survyr)
10 White William
11 Tubb Thomas
12 Jefferies John
13 Wright John
14 Timms Joseph
15 Wheeler William
16 Hutchins Thomas
17 Tyrrell Charles James
19 Lavis Mrs
20 Purbrick Mrs

Islip road (Summertown), from Hernes road.
NORTH SIDE.
3 Hopcroft Mrs
5 Johnson William
19 Lipscombe Mrs
35 Biovois Victor
65 Slay Mrs
67 Parsons Mrs
71 Amos John
73 Detlman Thomas
75 Bowerman Jesse
79 Soanes Joseph
SOUTH SIDE.
32 Mills William
34 Morris John
40 Morris Henry
42 Faulkner William
44 Cluzeaux Madame Chas, laundry (Biarritz cot)
50 Hall Frederick
52 HedgesWilliam,shopkpr
58 Casters Mrs
60 Innes Frederick
62 Busby William

James place(St.Clement's), from 23 Caroline street.
1 Allen Mrs
2 Penton Mrs
3 Hamilton Mrs
4 Collier William Charles
5 Smith George
6 Barrett Richard

James street (Cowley St. John), from 51 Iffley road.
1 Pole William
2 Gibson Mrs
3 Facer Mrs
4 Read Richard William
5 Allum John, boot maker
6 Allum Miss
7 Swadling John Charles
8 Cottrell Henry, baker
11 DoubledayR.D.inspector of weights & measures
12 Smith Miss
13 Lord Frank
14 Bacon Frederick
15 Barrington Walter
16 Pether Ernest
17 Higgs Francis John
18 Browne John
19 Kennah John Edward
20 Valters J.C.bookbinder
21 Turner John Richd.Fras

6*

Fig. 5.5 Kelly's Directory of Oxford, 1894/95

washing out to the laundries. The entries in the classified trades list include evidence that some laundries were using machinery, but others seem to claim that hand washing was better. It would also be possible to plot the location of these businesses on a map to see if they were mainly in the new smart suburbs or the working class areas of the town. The street directory (Figure 5.4) shows two of the largest in Islip Road in an area called Summertown, and comparison with an 1894/5 directory (Figure 5.5) suggests that the road was being newly developed at that time with only ten houses occupied, but Madame Cluzeaux at Biarritz Cottage has already started what became the French Laundry.

PROBLEMS

Possible difficulties using directories

The only warning to bear in mind when using commercial directories is to remember that they only provide part of the picture. Unlike the census returns which are official documents aiming to record everyone in the community, directories record only heads of households or businesses and may not include all of these. Because of the practical difficulties, the information was not always accurate or up to date. Comparison with a census of the same date will frequently show up discrepancies, and this can be used to provoke questions about the relative accuracy of both sources.

6 Inventories

BACKGROUND
What is an inventory?

The inventories referred to in this chapter are properly called probate inventories, or inventories post mortem (meaning "after death"). They are lists of a person's belongings and their values at the time of death and they date from the Tudor and Stuart periods, although they continued to be produced after that but become less useful for school purposes.

The law enforcing the making of an inventory was passed by parliament in Henry VIII's reign (in 1529). The purpose was to ensure that executors, and relatives who expected to benefit from the will, knew the value of the deceased's goods so that there could be no argument or fraud on either side. They are usually kept together with the person's will, and both had to be presented and "proved" in one of the church courts. This was usually in the local diocese, but if the will referred to property in more than one diocese it had to be proved in the Consistory Courts of Canterbury or York. Quite often, wealthy people chose to use these courts rather than the local one, even if their property was only local, perhaps because it implied a certain "status". The only people who did not have to have an inventory made were those whose goods were worth less than £5, but even some of these did.

The procedure for making an inventory was that four "honest persons", usually neighbours or respected members of the local community, had to go into the deceased person's house and list all the contents, the "goods and chattells", and place a value on them. This did not include the house itself, but only the contents, together with things like craft tools, farm implements, crops and livestock in fields and barns. It could also included the person's clothes and any cash, "ready money", in the house. Sometimes the appraisers, as they were called, got tired of listing every small item separately and simply wrote "and other lumber". The completed list was then signed by the appraisers either with a proper signature or with a mark.

Such a list of someone's possessions can reveal quite a lot about that person, their wealth, lifestyle and even about their house. Inventories are thus important in providing detailed information about daily life and standards of living in Tudor and Stuart times. The values of items cannot be taken as precise, but they do suggest the relative importance of various possessions and the totals give an indication of a person's wealth. The opening paragraph, which follows a standard form of words, often gives the person's occupation, so the economic standing of various crafts and trades can be seen.

The main interest, however, is simply to see what people had in their homes in Tudor and Stuart times, and no other record takes us so close to the ordinary people of that time.

An additional advantage is that many inventories list the contents room by room, naming each room as the appraisers go round the house. This can tell us a lot about 16th and 17th century houses – how many rooms they had, how they were arranged, and sometimes (from the contents) what they were used for. This may not be so obvious from the name: cooking was frequently done in the hall in older houses, and bed chambers were often used for storing unexpected items (like 46 cheeses in one example!). The once common routines of domestic baking and brewing, unfamiliar to most families today, are illustrated through the equipment listed.

WHERE?

Finding inventories

Inventories will be found in your local archives office, usually attached to the wills of the people whose possessions they list. Originally there would always have been a will and an inventory together, but by now one or other may have been lost. The number of inventories surviving varies from one place to another, but there should not be any problem in finding a local example. There are some published collections, and your archivist will be able to tell you whether any exist for your county.

You will also need the help of the archive office staff to locate a suitable example. Wills and inventories are catalogued under people's names, but you are probably not interested in any particular person and so will not have a name to search for in the catalogue. What you want is an inventory from the Tudor period which has some interesting detail – the person's occupation, names of rooms in the house, and perhaps a list of items associated with a craft or trade as well as farming activities – and one which is clearly written and not too difficult to read. Most archivists will be able, if you give them sufficient notice, to provide a few examples from which you can select the ones to use.

Most inventories are written on single sheets and are therefore usually suitable for photocopying so that copies of the originals as well as transcripts can be used by children in their own classroom.

HSUs

Inventories and the National Curriculum

Inventories are probably not suitable for KS1 work.

At KS2, they provide a fascinating source of information about people's homes in the 16th and 17th centuries. Their main use is therefore likely to be in connection with SU2 *Life in Tudor Times*, for which they clearly illustrate the living conditions and possessions of people at different levels of society. If sufficient suitable examples of inventories are available, a study of Tudor homes in the local area (perhaps also using surviving buildings) would make a good Local History Study Unit.

The way people wrote in the 16th century (and who could and could not write) is another interesting aspect of life in Tudor times which can be illustrated from inventories.

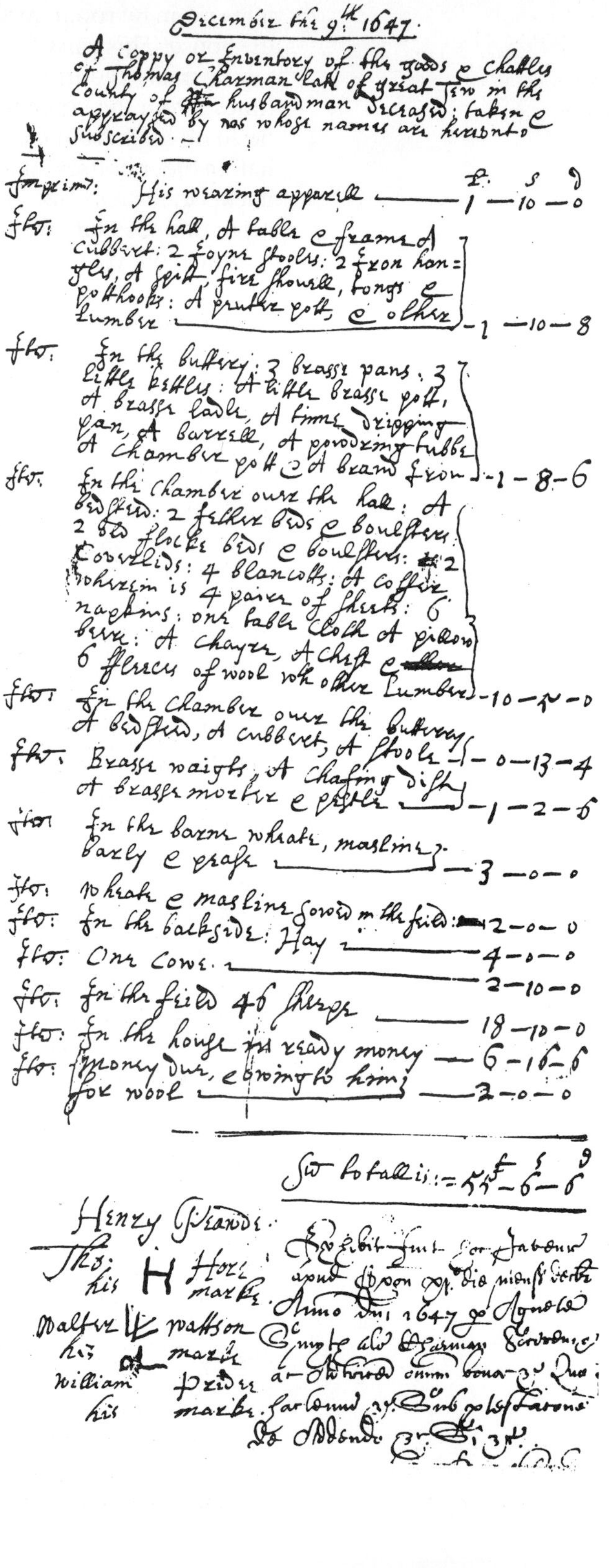

Fig. 6.1 Inventory of
Thomas Charman, 1649

Using inventories
*Focus on Tudor and
Stuart homes*

This example uses just one inventory, but the work could be expanded by having groups working on two or three different ones and comparing their findings. Having explained what an inventory is, start by letting children look at the copy of the original (Figure 6.1), to find their way around it and see what words they can work out for themselves. Discuss the way the list was made by the "appraysers" and find their names. Did they sign their names? Can you tell which one wrote this inventory? When was it made? Using both the original and a transcript they can then investigate the evidence through questions like the following, designed to focus attention on various aspects of a 17th century home as illustrated in the document (Figure 6.2).

❒ How many rooms were there in his house? What were they called?

❒ How were the rooms arranged? Draw a plan of his house.

❒ Where was the cooking done?

❒ How was meat roasted?

❒ Where were most of the pots and pans kept? What were they made of?

❒ What furniture did he have? How many beds, how many tables, how many chairs and stools?

December the 9th 1647
*A coppy or Inventory of the goods & chattles
of Thomas Charman late of Great Tew in the
county of Oxon. husbandman deceased: taken &
appraysed by us whose names are hereunto
subscribed.*

	£	s	d
Imprimis His wearing apparell	1	10	0
Item In the hall, A table & frame A cubbert: 2 joyne stooles: 2 Iron hangers, A spitt, fire shovell, tongs and pothooks: A pewter pott, other lumber	1	10	8
Item In the butterey: 3 brasse pans: 3 little kettles: A little brasse pott, A brasse ladle, a tinne dripping pan, a barrell, A powdering tubbe A Chamber pott & a brand iron	1	8	6
Item In the Chamber over the hall: A bedsteed: 2 fether beds & boulsters: 2 Coverlids: 4 blancotts: A Coffer wherein is 4 paier of sheets: 6 napkins: one table Cloth A pillow beere: A Chayer, A Chest & 6 Fleeces of wool with other lumber	10	5	0
Item In the Chamber over the butterey A bedsteed, A Cubbert, a stoole	0	13	4
Item Brasse waigts, A Chafing dish A brasse morter & pestle	1	2	6

Fig. *6.2 Transcript of the Inventory of Thomas Charman: evidence about his home*

17th century furniture could be illustrated from pictures, or better still by visiting museums with actual examples. Finding out what the house might have looked like would link with other work on buildings of this period, materials and styles, etc. Children could then draw pictures of Thomas Charman's home, or "furnish" each room with pictures of the contents.

A good follow-up is to get children to make their own "inventory" of the contents of some of the rooms in their home and to compare this with a 17th century home.

Jobs in Tudor and Stuart times

Many inventories give the person's occupation and list items like tools and equipment for that job. The inventory of Richard Skermer, weaver, of Upton in Nottinghamshire included:

> In the shop (workshop) double loom and geares (for broadcloth?) 1 warp fatt (vat for dyeing) with all materials fit for the trade ..... 3. 0. 0.

It also included cattle, pigs and stored wheat, barley and rye, showing that he, like many others at this time, did not rely on just one occupation.

Thomas Charman was described as "husbandman" – a small farmer – and children can investigate this through his inventory (Figure 6.3).

	£	s	d
Item In the barne wheate, masline barly & pease	3	0	0
Item Wheate & masline sowed in the feild	2	0	0
Item In the backside: Hay	4	0	0
Item One Cowe	2	10	0
Item In the Feild 46 sheepe	18	10	0
Item In the house in ready money	6	16	0
Item Money due & owing to him for wool	2	0	0
Sum totall is	55	6	6

Henry Peande

Tho   Hore
his   marke

Walter   Watson
his   marke

William   Pridee
his   marke

Fig. 6.3 *Transcript of the Inventory of Thomas Charman: evidence about his work*

❑ What crops did he grow?

❑ This inventory was made in December. What summer crops had been harvested?

❏ What winter crops were still growing?

❏ What animals did he keep?

❏ Which was worth more, a cow or a sheep?

❏ What do you think was the main thing he produced on his farm?

History of writing and printing

Inventories are interesting examples of 16th and 17th century hand-writing, quite apart from the information they contain. Because they were written by fairly ordinary people, often neighbours of the deceased, they are sometimes rather untidy examples of every-day work instead of the more formal "secretary hand" of official documents.

Children could be taught some of the letter shapes of the period and practise writing their names in this style. Quills, usually from geese, were the normal writing impements and could be improvised using other feathers if necessary. They could then try to read an inventory.

Not all archive offices have facilities for group visits by children, but if your's does then arrange for them to see some original inventories.

PROBLEMS

Possible difficulties using inventories

At first sight the handwriting may appear to be a problem – for teachers let alone children! Children will certainly need to have the document transcribed into modern typescript, but they should also see the original. Older pupils will be able to decipher some words for themselves and usually enjoy doing so. How much time they spend on this part of the activity depends on the teacher and on the nature of the document they are using.

For teachers the task of transcribing is not as daunting as it looks. When you look more closely, the writing often turns out to be not so difficult after all, and nearly all inventories use the same form of words and follow the same standard format, so that you soon know what to expect. There are some excellent books to help beginners read 16th and 17th century writing if you need them, and to read many inventories you will not need to become an expert. You may even manage without these books at all, but they will probably save you some time with unusual letter forms (see the Further Reading section on page 105). Although archive office staff should not be expected to transcribe the whole document, they will be very willing to help with the difficult words when you get stuck. The greatest problem will often be not the writing but the very erratic and phonetic spelling, and the archaic names of various bits of furniture or equipment found in the house. There are a number of books which deal with inventories and some of these contain glossaries of unusual terms which are a great help. Anyone who has made the effort to transcribe an inventory, with help from these sources, will discover the fascination of such documents for themselves.

7 Maps and air photographs

BACKGROUND

Maps

Maps, plans, charts, panoramas, even models vary in type and complexity. For the purposes of this book 'map' stands for all these types.

What is a map?

One definition is 'a representation of the disposition of anything'. It may be drawn or modelled to any scale, with its purpose to help the viewer visualise the full-sized reality. Thus a modern world atlas, and a child's sketch plan of the classroom are both maps.

Bear in mind that all maps leave out more than they put in.

History

Travellers on land and voyagers by sea drew the first maps, as aids to return to places they had found. Early and medieval plans were drawn showing towns and estates, to set down land ownership and define boundaries. Tudor and later maps were much more realistically drawn and dimensioned, giving more detail, but still often using local units of measurement.

Names on maps

The names on all these maps give clues as to what living in the places concerned must have been like. It may be hard to picture wildcats and wolves in the southern half of England, but the placenames Catford (London) and Woolmer (Hants) tell us they were there.

Local maps are a storehouse of information about people. For example, Cambridge Town, Surrey, was founded in 1862, and named after the Commander in Chief of the Army which was based there, the Duke of Cambridge. The name was later changed to Camberley.

Names also tell us about past occupiers. Teasdale's Yard, Alnwick, is typical of thousands of courtyard communities throughout the country; modern maps showing this particular street reflect the 1820s owner/occupier of the property.

Parish names were mostly old by the time of the Domesday Book (see the chapter 'Other sources'), and offer us information about owners and characteristics in the Saxon/Viking period.

Field names and farm names, however, may only date from the Tudor or later periods. Field names are sometimes remembered in today's street names, often in amended form. These names can give insights into (and pose questions about) community life. Although the common 'Bell field' may refer to the shape of a former field, it also commonly describes a field with produce that was reserved for the upkeep of the parish church bells. Names including 'Glebe' are of roads or properties on church land. Many place names situated round central communities (often now 'suburbs') reflect their original position on the edge of former waste land; for example names ending in -moor, -mere and -marsh.

County maps

A number of county maps were produced from the 16th century by well known cartographers like Saxton (34 counties mapped between 1574 and 79), Norden (1590s), Speed (1610 and later) and Morden (1690s). They frequently copied a predecessor's work, adding some new features, but also inheriting inaccuracies.

Such maps are interesting themselves as examples of Tudor and Stuart mapmaking, but have only limited use as local history evidence in the classroom, because they contain little detail. They illustrate the distribution of villages and towns (including once-

Fig. 7.1 Speed's bird's eye view plan of Hull, 1610

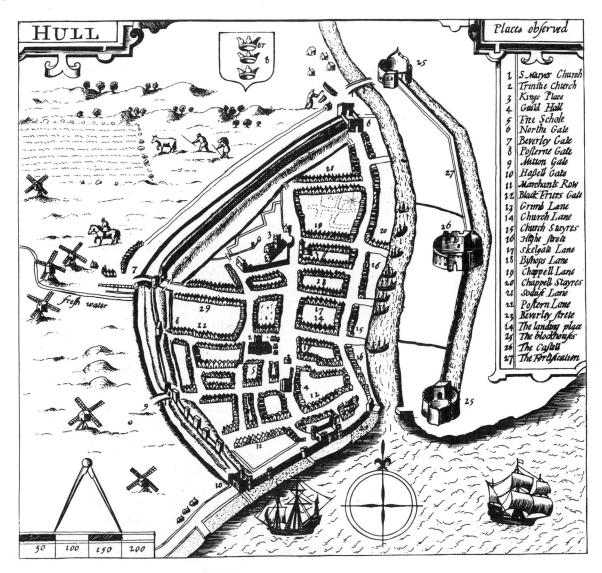

isolated villages now swallowed up by towns and cities) and early forms of place names. While roads were often not shown, the maps do show the location of the forests which were much more extensive in the 16th and 17th centuries than today.

The 18th century saw another spate of mapmaking, often on a much larger scale, and therefore more useful in school. Nearly every county in England and Wales had a new survey made of it, by men like Jefferys, Rocque and Evans; but many were done by local amateur surveyors. They vary considerably in accuracy and it may be possible to check features like field boundaries against other large-scale maps, and discuss the reliability of these as historical sources (AT3). These maps often show details of importance to a local study, such as turnpike roads, tollgates, windmills and watermills as they existed 200 years ago.

Many new and reprinted editions of county maps continued to appear in the 19th century, but undoubtedly the best maps from this period were produced by the Ordnance Survey (see below).

Estate maps

Estate maps are very useful if one exists for your parish. As opposed to earlier written descriptions, estate maps were produced in increasing numbers from about 1570 onwards, and about 30,000 still exist up and down the country. They generally show the land owned by the person or institution who commissioned the map, concentrating on field boundaries, acreages and field or furlong names (for an adapted example, see Figure 7.7 below). Occasionally, they may show streets or even buildings in the village.

Town plans

Early town plans, to various scales, were published locally in Tudor times and earlier. They often took the form of panoramas or birds-eye views. Several 17th and 18th century cartographers added town plans to their county maps (see Figure 7.1). In the 18th and 19th centuries, very detailed and large scale plans were published (e.g. Richard Horwood's 1792-99 plan of London to 26 inch : 1 mile scale (see Figure 7.2)).

Enclosure and tithe-award maps

Between about 1760 and 1840, much of the farmland and wasteland in lowland Britain, previously arranged in open fields and managed by a communal system, was enclosed into smaller fields alloted to individual owners and tenants. In each parish where this happened, an Act of Parliament had to be passed, and surveyors were appointed to measure the land, re-allocate it, and draw up an award document and a large-scale map of the new fields and their owners. Many of these enclosure maps survive, and contain interesting information about the layout of the parish. They may not contain much detail about buildings in the village.

The Tithe Commutation Act (1836) formalised an annual cash payment to replace the ancient payments of one tenth part of people's produce (and labour). This commutation involved producing large scale maps of the whole parish, accompanied by lists of landowners and occupiers, showing their holdings of the relevant land.

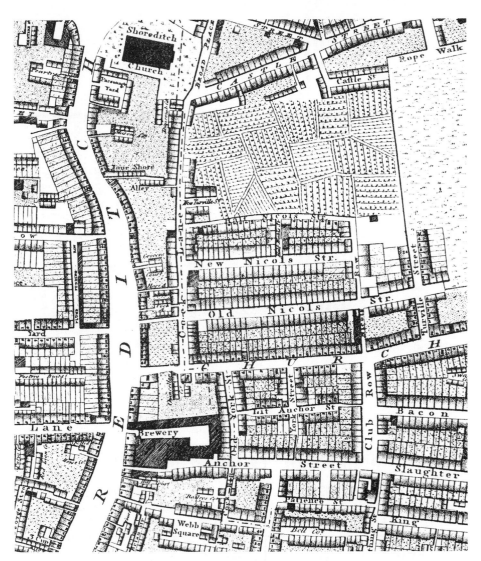

Fig. 7.2 *Part of Richard Horwood's London plan, showing Shoreditch*

Three copies of these documents were made. The number of counties in England affected by this act was roughly the same as for enclosures, though there were fewer in the north.

The problem with both types of map is their large size and the impossibility of copying them except by photography (ask your librarian: photographs or tracings may have been taken).

Transport maps

Many maps in all periods were produced to assist travellers, and some of the most useful at KS2 and KS3 are John Ogilby's road maps produced in the late 17th century. These show a hundred of the major routes in England, mapped in an unusual strip form. They show all the features a 17th and 18th century traveller would need to know: mileages, side roads, hills, bridges, fords, and towns and villages on the route. Other mapmakers copied Ogilby's format, such as the one by Edward Mogg, whose maps were accompanied with a detailed itinerary (see Figure 7.3).

Published by E. MOGG, N° 14, Great Russell Street, Covent Garden,

A SURVEY
OF THE
HIGH ROADS OF ENGLAND & WALES,
WITH
PART OF SCOTLAND,

Planned on a Scale of One Inch to a Mile; exhibiting, at one view, the Seats of the Nobility and Gentry, whether situated on, or contiguous to the Roads; the various branches of Roads, and Towns to which they lead; together with the actual distance of the same from the main Road; the Rivers, Navigable Canals, Railways, Turnpike Gates, &c. &c.; and annexed to each Town or Village the names of such Inns as supply Post Horses. To which is added, a General Index, containing a brief Description of each Place, Seat, or remarkable object, in the Work. The First Part, comprising the Southern Division of the Kingdom, embellished with a handsome Vignette Title, is now complete, and ready for delivery. Price £4.4s. half-bound, Russia.

*** For the convenience of pleasure Tourists, detached portions of the above beautiful Work, forming separate and distinct Roads, may be had at the Prices annexed.*

No.	ROADS.	£	s.	d.
1.	LONDON to DOVER	0	2	6
2.	LONDON to DOVER, including Margate	0	3	0
3.	LONDON to HASTINGS	0	3	6
4.	LONDON to PORTSMOUTH	0	3	0
5.	LONDON to PORTSMOUTH, including the road to Chichester, through Haslemere and Midhurst...	0	4	0
6.	LONDON to PORTSMOUTH, including the road to Chichester, through Petworth	0	4	0
7.	LONDON to PORTSMOUTH and CHICHESTER, including the roads to Bognor, Arundel, and Little Hampton	0	5	0
8.	LONDON to BRIGHTON, through Reigate, Crawley, and Cuckfield	0	2	6
9.	LONDON to BRIGHTON, through Croydon, East Grinstead and Lewes	0	2	6
10.	LONDON to WORTHING, through Epsom, Leatherhead, Dorking, and Horsham	0	2	6
11.	LONDON to SOUTHAMPTON, through Staines, Bagshot, Basingstoke, and Winchester	0	3	6
12.	LONDON to SOUTHAMPTON, through Staines, Bagshot, Basingstoke, and Winchester; and also through Farnham, Alton, and Alresford; with branches to Poole, through Wimborne Minster; to Lymington, through Lyndhurst; to Christchurch, through Ringwood; and to Gosport, through Fareham.............................	0	10	0
13.	LONDON to EXETER, through Basingstoke, Andover, Salisbury, Blandford, Dorchester, Bridport, Axminster, and Honiton	0	7	6
14.	No. 13 continued, to Plymouth and Devonport, through Chudleigh and Ashburton, and thence to Falmouth, through Liskeard, Lostwithiel, and Truro	0	10	0
15.	LONDON to EXETER, through Basingstoke, Stockbridge, Salisbury, Shaftesbury, Sherborne, Axminster, Chard, and Honiton	0	8	0

346

LONDON TO BUNGAY, CONTINUED TO NORWICH. BY SAXMUNDHAM and HALESWORTH.

MEASURED from WHITECHAPEL CHURCH.

	From Norwich	From London
Tumbledown Dick	9¼	114
Kirstead Hall	6¾	116½
Poringland	4½	118¼
Poringland Heath, *Windmill*	3¼	119½
Bixley	2¼	120¼
½ m. farther, you join the road from Beccles, through Loddon.		
To Beccles 14¾ m.		
Trowse Turnpike	1¼	122
Cross the Yare		
* NORWICH, Market Place		123¾

crosses; the top of one of them being adorned with a figure of Astræa, in lead, weighing 15cwt. The principal streets are broad, well paved, and lighted; they branch out from the market-place at the great road leading to Norwich, Yarmouth, Bury, Ipswich, Beccles, and Lowestoft, and being each terminated by a handsome structure, convey, at first sight a very favourable impression. The fine and spacious assembly-room are near buildings, and the county bridge over the Waveney is of modern erection: here is also a free grammar-school, and a meeting-house. Contiguous to the town is an inclosed common of great extent and fertility; and a pleasant walk of about a mile and a half to the lower end of it, leads to the Bath-house, where there is an excellent cold-bath: the town has also several springs yielding a strong mineral water; but one of them in particular, at the King's Head Inn, is said to possess medicinal properties of great efficacy. A considerable trade is carried on in corn, malt, flour, coal, lime, &c. by means of the river Waveney, which almost surrounds the town and common, in the form of a horseshoe; and several capital flour-mills, malting-offices, lime-kilns, &c. have also been recently erected. Here is likewise a manufactory of Suffolk hempen cloth. Market on Thursday.

LONDON TO DUNWICH, THROUGH WOODBRIDGE.

MEASURED from WHITECHAPEL CHURCH.

	From Dunwich	From London
From Whitechapel Church to * WOODBRIDGE, Suffolk, page 342	97¼	20¼
Cross the river Deben		
Eyke	16¼	80¾
Rendlesham	15¼	81¼
Tunstall	12¼	84¼
Snape Bridge	10¼	87
Cross the river Alde		
2¼ m. farther, To Aldborough 4 m. to Saxmundham 3½ m. London to * ALDBOROUGH 93½ m.		
Leiston	5½	91¾
* DUNWICH		97¼

RENDLESHAM, Loudham Hall, *James Macdonald, Esq.*; Rendlesham House, *Lord Rendlesham*; and Naunton Hall, *Rev. — Naunton.*
LEISTON, 2 m. beyond, Theberton Hall, *Col. Sondes.*
DUNWICH stands on a cliff of considerable height, commanding an extensive view of the German ocean, and was at one time an important, opulent, and commercial city; but is now a place of little consideration, though it still retains its weekly market, held on Monday, and has sent two members to Parliament, ever since the commons of England first acquired the right of representation. This town is thought to have been a station of the Romans, but is certainly a place of high antiquity, and was made a bishop's see in the early part of the seventh century: its present ruinous condition is chiefly owing to the repeated encroachments of the ocean; and being seated on a hill composed of loam and sand of a loose texture, on a coast destitute of rocks, it is not surprising that its buildings should have successively yielded to the impetuosity of the billows. Dunwich formerly contained several parish churches, but they are all entirely destroyed, except that of All Saints, of which the square tower is still pretty entire, though nothing remains of the body of the edifice, unless it be a portion of the outer walk.

ALDBOROUGH. The Marine Villa, *Lewson Vernon, Esq.*; *Hon. Percy C. Wyndham, Esq.*; *Sir George Wombwell, Bart.*; and *Col. Carnac.*
LEISTON, Leiston Old Abbey, *Wm. Tatnall, Esq.*

** *The best Roads to Aldborough, and Dunwich, will be found at page 342.*

LONDON TO ORFORD, THROUGH WOODBRIDGE.

MEASURED from WHITECHAPEL CHURCH.

	From Orford	From London
From Whitechapel Church to Melton Turnpike, Suffolk, page 342	89¼	11½
Cross the river Deben		
Bromeswell	10	79¾
Sprat Bridge	8	81¼
Butley, *The Oyster*	5½	84¼
Chillesford	4¼	85¼
Sudbourn	2	87¾
ORFORD		89¼

ORFORD, situated near the confluence of the rivers Alde and Ore, is a small and ill-built, but corporate town, sending two members to parliament, though it is not, a parish, the church being only a chapel of ease to the adjacent village of Sudbourn. The object here most deserving notice is the castle, seated on a rising ground, that is reported to have been near the centre of the town; the only existing remains, however, of this edifice is the keep. The interior of this considerable strength, and the structure, itself forms a necessary sea-mark, especially for ships coming from Holland. Orford contains a mean town-hall, and a plain brick-built assembly-house, which latter structure was erected about half a century since.

BUTLEY. The ruins of the Abbey.
SUDBOURN, Sudbourn Hall, *Marquis of Hertford*, is a plain quadrangular edifice, covered with white composition, and was rebuilt by Wyatt about 40 years ago; the staircase is executed with blue and red bases; but the general appearance of simplicity rather than elegance; and it is mostly used as a sporting residence, the neighbourhood abounding with game.

Fig. 7.3 Edward Mogg's 1826 edition of Paterson's Roads, showing itineraries from London to the East coast; and a page from his catalogue of maps

Special maps for cyclists (often with warnings about steep hills), and for boating on rivers like the Thames, were produced in the late 19th and early 20th centuries. Other transport maps included those for turnpike roads, canals and railways. These vary in scale and in the amount of detail they show apart from the main route itself.

Ordnance Survey

War with France, and the need for accurate information about the countryside and its defence, led to the full survey of the whole country by the Board of Ordnance, using the latest scientific equipment and methods. The original project was founded in 1791 (called the 'Trigonometrical Survey'), and the first 1 inch maps* were ordered in 1797. This 'Old Series' finally consisted of 110 sheets,

Fig. 7.4 *Ordnance Survey 50 inch map of part of Hull*

* We give maps scales as 1 inch; 6 inch; 25 inch; 50 inch; 126 inch, though in fact the scales are these days quoted as 1:63,360; 1:10,560; 1:2500; 1:1250; 1:500.

and was published between 1801 and 1873.

A new edition (the 'New Series') was begun before the old one was completed, and its 300 sheets were issued between 1840 and 1860. Later editions followed. In all editions, minor amendments were made for different printings.

By 1855, plans were made for 'all cultivated districts' to be covered by 25 inch maps; and all towns with 4000 or higher populations by 126 inch maps. Today, the largest scale produced for general consumption is 50 inch, and all towns with a revised population of over 20,000 are covered (see Figure 7.4).

However, the way the Ordnance Survey is presenting these large-scale maps is changing. Instead of maps that provide 'complete' coverage, the use of sophisticated equipment allows maps to be produced to customers' individual specifications. So, if all you need is the immediate area around your school, you define the scale and area you need, and Ordnance Survey generates a map specially for you. Such maps are not cheap, but neither are they (relatively) more expensive than the range of other large-scale maps.

Special maps

The Ordnance Survey – and many other publishers, often with maps based on the Ordnance Survey – produce specialist maps and plans. These cover specific subjects (for example, geology), and periods (such as Roman Britain). See the Bibliography for a list of the most appropriate titles. In addition many 'utility' maps (showing plans of railways, electricity areas, and so on) have been produced; many of which are of great help in local studies.

Air photographs
History

The first air photographs were taken from balloons at the beginning of the 20th century, and aeroplanes were used during the 1914-18 war to take reconnaisance photographs of the enemy lines. In the course of this work, and even more so during post-war training flights, air force pilots began to take an interest in the earthworks and other historical sites clearly visible from the air.

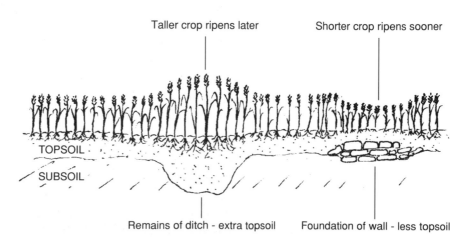

Fig. 7.5 How cropmarks are formed. Air photographs reveal the patterns made either by shadows from the taller or shorter crops, or the cropmarks caused by the differences in colour from earlier or later ripening than the rest of the field

Taller crop ripens later   Shorter crop ripens sooner

TOPSOIL

SUBSOIL

Remains of ditch - extra topsoil   Foundation of wall - less topsoil

The importance of this new perspective on history was realised by O.G.S. Crawford of the Ordnance Survey, who with other pilots encouraged the systematic use of aerial photography to record crop marks caused by buried features such as walls and ditches (see Figure 7.5). Since the 1920s, thousands of previously unknown archaeological sites have been discovered all over the country through this technique (for example the deserted medieval village of Muscott, near Northampton, Figure 7.6); and aerial photography is now a major tool of archaeological investigation.

Today, the whole country is covered by several complete series of photographs, produced both by official bodies and by commercial firms. The photographs are taken from directly overhead and from different angles.

Fig. 7.6 *Air photographs are particularly effective at providing evidence about historic features in the landscape. The details of this deserted village site in Northamptonshire could be used to investigate the layout of the village and its fields, as well as the reasons for its desertion*
(Cambridge Collection of Air Photographs: copyright reserved)

WHERE?

Finding maps and air photographs

Your main reference library will carry a wide selection of maps covering your area. You will be allowed to make photocopies (but you will be asked to sign a statement about their use for educational purposes).

Atlases of your county's old maps may have been reproduced, and individual maps will probably have been reprinted too. These you may be able to buy or borrow from your local library. The county record office will contain original maps, but these are not accessible for class use (and their size may present problems too). Detailed shopping plans have been produced by C Goad Limited for larger towns.

The 'Old Series' of Ordnance Survey 1 inch:1 mile maps have been reprinted and can be bought for a very modest sum at most bookshops. These are not in their original state (in other words they have had some amendments made since their very first printing), but this works to the advantage of KS2/3 teaching: the state chosen for reproduction includes the addition of early railways.

Contact any Ordnance Survey agent about their range of maps. Ask for their educational catalogue.

Air photographs can be bought from sources such as: Wildgoose Publications, (The Reading Room, Dennis Street, Hugglescote, LE67 2FP), and Aerofilms Limited (Gate Studios, Station Road, Boreham Wood, Herts WD6 1EJ). Your local library and record office will probably hold local examples, and may be able to copy these for you.

Making your own maps

Apart from the NC advantages for work in geography, mathematics, etc., producing maps is fun. A group of children studying one locality can present information clearly and concisely in this form. It is possible to instil a sense of adventure in presenting a blank or outline map for the class to fill in as things are discovered.

HSUs

Maps and the National Curriculum

At KS1, maps make useful illustrations of travellers' explorations.

For KS2 early estate and town maps, where they exist, can promote some exciting work on the locality in Tudor times, but it is more likely that maps will be used in connection with *Victorian Britain* or a local history Unit dealing with the 19th of 20th centuries. The early editions of the Ordnance Survey maps are essential for looking at the changes in local towns and villages in Victorian times and the study of travel and transport, by road, railway or canal, should also make use of contemporary maps.

In addition there are some historial maps created by the Ordnance Survey which can be used as a source for *Romans, Anglo Saxons and Vikings in Britain*. (See the Further Reading section at the end of this book.)

ACTIVITIES

Using maps and air photographs

As with most sources, maps and air photographs should be used in close conjunction with other sources. Research in directories and censuses, for example, will be enhanced by looking at contemporary maps, and making your own maps of what you see in those sources will help you to understand them better.

1. Groups could discuss the reasons why different maps were made. One group could look at a medieval chart; another at a railway or tube map; a third at an estate or tithe map. Others could look at a d.i.y map of, say, a cub or brownie camping area; a geological or historical or leisure map; and so on. Each group could then report to the class on the different reasons. (This activity is particularly relevant to the skill of assessing data.)

2. Using an estate map, see what field names suggest about the way of life in the period concerned. For example, the 18th century Buckinghamshire plan (Figure 7.7) contains the following names. See if the class can find out what they originally meant:

Stocklands	[Cleared from wasteland.]
Hither Woodcock	[Where that bird would have been found; find out what sort of field this must have been (low-lying and wet).]
Ridings	[Another name meaning 'cleared from wasteland'.]
Grubbing	[A field from which scrub has been cleared.]
Halfway House Field	[The allusion is to the distances between Hughenden and High Wycombe.]
Little Millfield	[There is no mill here, but the class should be able to see where it was.]
Six o'clock Hill	[The map is faithfully draw with north at the top; the class may be able to deduce something of the lie of the land. This field is in fact up the side of a hill, with Tinker's Wood on the skyline, and indeed the sun would be blocked out from this field, making work in it difficult after 6pm quite early in the autumn.]

This activity can usefully lead to discussions on the kind of work that went on in farms; on the way the farm encroached on the wasteland; and on the effectiveness of a farm to support its owner and family.

3. Draw a map of your area on which to plot the results of your own local research.

IT graphics will help. This can then be used as the basis on which to plot, for example:

a) surviving buildings from different periods

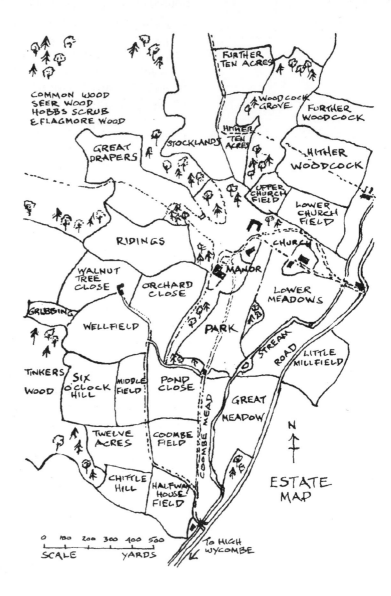

Fig. 7.7 Based on an estate map of Hughenden, Buckinghamshire

b) directory entries for particular trades

c) town growth

d) communications

e) journeys between homes and work; bride's and bridegroom's home parishes

and so on.

4. Produce a detailed map of what your area must have looked like in the period you are studying. Perhaps your map could be in the map-making style of the period.

IT

Investigating maps and air photographs

Mapping software

Concept keyboards, maps and air photographs

Information technology can assist in the study of local maps and air photographs in a number of ways. There are several mapping programs which allow pupils to plot individual records on a prepared base map. Information retrieval programs which work with a concept keyboard can also be used to investigate local maps and photographs, and a number of programs are very suitable for children to create their own maps.

Mapping software allows pupils to investigate the spatial relationships between aspects of local data, such as the location of buildings dating from different periods or those constructed from different materials in their local community. Such software might also be used to identify which areas of a town were most susceptible to epidemic diseases such as the plague or cholera or to investigate towns of birth from census returns.

The use of mapping software involves the creation of a base map and a data file of records for use with the map. Each record will contain a number of details about, for example, a particular building or individual, as well as a grid reference or location to link the record to its location on the base map. Children can then use the mapping software to plot the records on the base map, by asking questions and plotting different records in different colours or with various symbols. In this way, children can investigate the development of their local community by looking at the dates of buildings or the materials from which they were constructed; or they might compare the numbers of men, women and children affected by a particular epidemic in different parts of a town. Mapping software can also typically be used to produce a choropleth shading (an indication of the density or number of records falling within different grids across the map) of particular aspects of the data. In addition, such information can be presented graphically in the form of pie charts or bar charts for data at specific locations.

The base map will often need to be created by the teacher. Children, however, can collect the evidence for the data file of records and create it themselves. This information might come from a local survey of buildings, for example, or from the census returns or local records of an epidemic, etc. Children also need to use a contemporary map to identify the grid reference or location of each individual record in the data file. Clearly one of the keys to using mapping software of this kind is the ability to identify a particular location for each record to be included in the data file.

Concept keyboards* provide an alternative means of investigating maps, air photographs and pictures. A local map can be placed on the concept keyboard, for example, and when the children press

---

* A concept keyboard is an alternative means of entering information into a computer. It consists of an A4 or A3 pad connected to the computer with a touch sensitive surface over which can be laid a map, air photograph or picture. The software which accompanies the concept keyboard can then be "programmed" to respond with certain information when a particular part of the map or picture is touched. Concept keyboards are widely used by very young pupils or those with special educational needs.

the map the computer will provide information; or a question requiring some additional research; or a suggestion for an additional task about that particular location – whatever the teacher wants. Typically, a concept keyboard may contain up to 128 squares and some software, such as Touch Explorer Plus, allows the creation of several levels of information for each square. Thus, level one might simply contain some information, level two might contain a straightforward question, level three a more demanding question, etc. Alternatively, each of the levels can relate to a particular period in history. Children might thus investigate the changing use of buildings on a local map over a period of a hundred years, or the changing land use over a period of time from an air photograph. See Chapter 11 on photographs and pictures for more information about this particular application.

Graphics programs

Almost every school will have some graphics programs with which the children can create their own local maps. These might be 'drawn' freehand with a painting-type program, or very precisely with drawing programs (CAD – Computer Aided Design). Use of CAD will involve children in conducting research and taking precise measurements so that the finished map will be accurately scaled.

Alternatively, the class might use LOGO and 'turtle graphics' to produce a map of their classroom or a local area. Again this would involve research and precise measurements, and then the children would build procedures (a series of instructions) to teach the turtle how to draw the map. This type of activity can be carried out successfully with groups of children collaborating to produce different portions of the map. Provided that each group uses the same scale and orientation, they can produce separate procedures which are then linked together to make the final map. Procedures can also be created to put the classroom furniture in the right place!

PROBLEMS
Possible difficulties using maps

1. Availability of local maps in sufficient detail in your period. The physical size of some maps. The rarity of some maps, so that copying is not possible.

2. Bias in the mapmaker. Even good mapmakers made mistakes; there were limitations in the techniques available to them; and, above all, the maps were made with a particular market in mind, so political bias is likely.

3. Changes of placename/fieldname/etc. over time. People from one age tend to imagine modern words when using a past name they do not understand. For example, there is a farm in Buckinghamshire which in early Ordnance Survey maps is entered as Heartyfine Farm. This same name today appears as Hard-to-Find Farm.

8 Newspapers

BACKGROUND
The development of newspapers

Until the eighteenth century there were few newspapers as we think of them (apart from a prolific outburst when controls were swept away during the Civil War). Broadsheets were published which described specific events or supported particular political parties. Some provincial newspapers were produced in the pre-Victorian era, but only *The Times* commanded national sales.

Stamp duty was imposed upon newspapers in the pre-1855 period (4d – about £2 today – was the maximum figure). This helped to restrict readership to the rich, though libraries offered newspapers to their readers in the early nineteenth century.

Because of these shortcomings, the value of newspapers as a source for local information is limited until the second half of the nineteenth century.

In 1855, however, stamp duty on newspapers was repealed. Coupled with the improvement in public literacy, the development of printing machinery and railway distribution systems, this opened the way for mass newspapers. The *Daily Mail* was the first (founded 1896), and several others were established shortly afterwards.

The newsagent in a provincial town in the first half of the twentieth century would be able to offer one or more local newspapers, a small number of quality papers, and a strong selection of more popular ones (as well as weeklies). Their turnover of papers was high (the national circulation of newspapers was three million copies in 1918); but much higher in the second quarter of the century – the pre-TV period – when the total circulation was over 100 million copies per day.

For the National Curriculum, national newspapers offer particular viewpoints on important events (influenced by their political leanings). Our present concern, though, is in the reporting of local events as examples of national topics. So it is on the value of provincial newspapers as a source that we concentrate.

What do newspapers cover?

a) Nationally important events

The material that may be included is almost endless. A number of broad categories are suggested:

The devastating air raids on the city of Coventry in November 1940 are one example where the coverage will have been even more extensive and in greater detail in the local press than the many columns of coverage in the national newspapers. The opening of the extension of the Great Central Railway line from Nottingham to London between 1893 and 1899 benefited many different areas through which the line passed. But if you live on that route, your local papers will have covered the opening with particular intensity and interest for a local study. The hunger march to London from the North East of England in 1936 was extensively covered nationally; but more space will have been devoted to it by the local press of Jarrow and of the towns through which the march passed.

Fig. 8.1 *How different sections of the community spent Christmas in 1871 (The Birmingham Daily Post, 26th December)*

ıring the
requiring
nake the
tomimes.
esses of
he house
dramatic
." The
vourable
n that of
: Beard,"
. upon a
pted at
trong in
boastful
Thumb"
heatres"
lay and
Gilbert's
ıristmas.
: Queen's
Days of
and dra-
aturday.
accord-
the new
ery part
drop the
u desire
agueness
isitors to
of the re-
-"Please
ou mean
the play
dramatis
e limited
utionary
the piece
enever a
oduces a
failure.
e It" for
ane, on
as Rosa-
lay-going
ot go to
slovenly
may be.
A good
ound by
ry other
er, agree
: general
m to act
ness and
at the
ithin the
an equal
lequately
ıeatre of
company
a play of
t draw as
mping."
nsational
ght, with
White,"
od. The
in "The
Bateman's

the care taken by the body that is supposed to govern the streets, we pass on to notice how Christmas was kept at the public institutions.

THE WORKHOUSE.

At this great institution, which has a population of nearly 2,?00 persons, Christmas was celebrated in the good old traditional style. A general relaxation of discipline was permitted, greatly to the joy of the inmates, and not a little increasing the labours and anxieties of the officials, who good humouredly submitted to the extra strain. A mighty distribution of beef and plum pudding took place at dinner time, and the four or five hundred chubby, hearty, healthy children set to work in a way that was appetising to witness. The house was decorated with greenery, festoons, and Chinese lanterns; and the chapel was tastefully and appropriately ornamented. In the afternoon a brass band attended and performed to the inmates, and a conjuring entertainment was given by Professor Greatway. Oranges and nuts were given to the children, and the Messrs. Baker, of Granville Street, made their usual donation of 2d. to every child over two years of age. The older people who knew what to do with such luxuries, received some tobacco and snuff, and the women enjoyed an extra indulgence in the way of tea, so that it may be taken for granted that gossip flowed in abundant streams. At night the officials had a ball.

THE BOROUGH LUNATIC ASYLUM.

The inmates of this institution have had their usual entertainments at this festive season. On Saturday the recreation hall, which had been decorated with evergreens, holly, and mistletoe for the occasion, was filled by about four hundred of the patients. The time was occupied in singing, dancing, jingling matches, &c. Fruit was distributed during the evening amongst the inmates, who, as a rule, appeared to greatly enjoy what took place around them. At 9.30 they had supper. Yesterday they had a dinner of roast beef and plum pudding, and nothing was left undone by Mr. Green and Mr. Knight which could contribute to their enjoyment.

THE BOROUGH GAOL.

Those of the "shrewd" criminals who smiled to themselves under the impression that incarceration in the Borough Gaol secured a Christmas dinner of roast beef and plum pudding must, yesterday, have felt not a little disappointment. If they had a large sense of humour they probably laughed at finding that their cunning had been outwitted even by Visiting Justices. These gentlemen do not approve of petty thefts being encouraged by the prospect of a good dinner, and consequently no change was made in the gaol diet on Christmas Day.

THE HOSPITALS.

Yesterday, the inmates at the General and the Queen's Hospitals were provided with dinners of roast beef and plum puddings. At the General Hospital, in the evening, there were Christmas trees loaded with countless articles. The wards at each institution were tastefully decorated.

THE CHILDREN'S HOSPITAL.

The little inmates of this Hospital could not, of course, keep Christmas with the proper festivity of diet, for careful diet is a part of the means of cure. But the wards were decorated with laurel and holly, in addition to the pictures and ornaments which customarily give them such a cheerful appearance. In one ward was a Christmas tree. Toys were plentifully supplied, and the parents or friends of the little ones were allowed to visit them, as on an ordinary Monday.

CHRISTMAS ENTERTAINMENTS.

There is no lack of amusements this Christmas, and as there is certainly no lack of persons who are craving to be amused, we anticipate overflowing houses at all the places whose cheery doors invite the public to step in and enjoy themselves. The highly satisfactory condition in which the local trade has been for some time past may be supposed to have placed a good deal of coin in circulation, and as, when things go prosperously, those who amuse the public well are rewarded with liberal liberality, our entertainers may be congratulated upon their prospects. Tastes differ—so do the means of gratifying them. Here is a list from which to choose :—

THE PANTOMIMES.

Another turn of the wheel of Old Time and Boxing Day—the glorious "season" of juvenalia—once more brings us those amusements and entertainments which are as en-

with preparations for the wedding of the Dwarf and Goody, the appearance of the Squire and his party, and the retrieval of the fortunes of the day. Scene 9 gives the fairies and a fairy glade. Yellow Grain expresses his delight at having won the day, and sings a song. John, the lover of Goody, is told by Spiteful that his lady-love is down a coalmine with the dwarf; and in Scene 10 we have a combat, "Down among the coals," in which everything comes right, and everybody is made happy; the triumph of the shield of truth over the powers of darkness is revealed in the transformation scene, "The Temple of Jupiter." The pantomime will, undoubtedly, maintain the reputation of this theatre for the splendour and beauty with which former pantomimes have been produced. Miss Bella Goodall, from the Royal Strand Theatre, will take the character of Colin; Miss Kate Hastings, that of Goody-two-Shoes; Mr. Mervin, of Mrs. Wood's St. James's Company, that of Rumbuskin; and Miss Nellie Smith, that of Squire Yellow Graine Harlequin is Mr. Talleen Welch; Columbine, Mdlle. Ernestine; Pantaloon, Mr. Harry Green; and Clown, M. Nicolo Deulin. The entire pantomime will be producd. under the immediate superintendence of Mr. James Rodgers and Mr. Strachan.

BIRMINGHAM CONCERT HALL.

It may truly be said that the lover of Christmas amusements is at the present time *embarras de richesses*. Among those who make up their minds to visit all the best places of entertainment, the Birmingham Concert Hall will receive, if not first, at any rate, very early attention. The enterprising managers have spared no pains both to please the public and gain for themselves a satisfactory return. On the list of artistes engaged for the holiday week, Mr. G. Fredericks and Miss Carrie Julian stand first. Then there are also Mr. W. West, negro-comedian; Mr. H. Bolton, comedian; Mr. E. A. Hart, comic vocalist; Mr. F. Ford, comedian; and Mr. Artois, gymnast. In addition to the foregoing, five charming female vocalists have been engaged. The most attractive feature of the entertainment, however, is the new comic spectacular ballet, entitled "Ethenia, Fairy of the Silver Star, and Little Boy Blue; or, the Ogre of the Enchanted Castle." We may safely predict a crowded house, both this evening and throughout the Christmas holidays.

DAY'S CONCERT HALL.

Judging from the programme which Mr. James Day has issued, there has been a determination on his part that not only should his Christmas entertainment maintain the reputation which his establishment has gained in previous years, but that it should, if possible, add to it. The Christmas ballet "Jack o'Lantern," upon which so much care has been bestowed will be produced this evening. We published a sketch of the plot last week, and all that we need do now is to state that the ballet scene and the transformation scene are extremely beautiful. The latter is intended to represent the marine abode of some mythical young ladies called fairies, or naiads, or mermaids, at the bottom of the sea. It is resplendent with glittering shells, and when brought into strong relief by the lime light the effect is dazzling. Sea nymphs glide upon the scene, or rise apparently from the depths of the sea; in a nautilus shell a beauteous "naughty lass" descends, and all around are sea anemones, sea-weeds, and shells of every hue. The dresses are very showy—gold and silver—and each fairy has a fanciful head-dress resembling a large open brightly polished shell. There are other accessories which help to make a scene so brilliant and so effective that it must ensure the success of the ballet. We may mention that Miss d'Este plays the leading part. The ordinary company comprises the Great Saphrini, a clever impersonator of both male and female character; and Mr. Richard Durden, Miss A. Raynham, and Miss E. Bower, old favourites in the serio-comic line. Mr. Fox Ray, Miss Stilliard, and Mrs. Fellows complete the list of *artistes*.

MUSEUM CONCERT HALL.

At this establishment there is a very attractive "bill o fare" for the Christmas holidays. Mr. Biber, with his usual enterprise, has secured a talented company, which includes *artistes* whose names at once guarantee mirth and entertainment to the full. This evening, Mr. and Mrs. Langon, and "Joe" Millicent, who are known to the Birmingham public in connection with this hall as good negro vocalists, comedians, and dancers, again appear on the boards. Mr. and Mrs. Mark Dearlove, comedians, have also been engaged, and though it is now some time since they last appeared at this establishment they will probably fully revive the popularity-

b) Local news

Sometimes what is reported in a provincial town is part of a national upheaval (e.g. the Swing riots). Sometimes it is symptomatic of a country-wide problem (cholera outbreaks caused by poor drainage and water supply). Often, though, it covers just the same day-to-day events that may be read in local papers today: a charabanc overturns in 1937 at a busy crossroads; a river breaks its banks and floods a row of houses; a house is demolished following a gas explosion; a major river freezes over. On a community basis, the opening of public buildings, churches, bridges, parks, etc. are covered in great detail. Political meetings are reported at length. Society weddings include descriptions amounting to many column inches on every aspect – often listing all the guests and what they gave the happy couple! Sporting occasions, including meets of the local hunt are covered. Celebrations and entertainments are reviewed, such as those shown in Figure 8.1. These are just a few of the routine events of every country town and village.

c) Advertisements and notices

As with many of the categories listed above, the advertisements to be found in historic newspapers are not so very different from the same sort of papers today. This rich source of information about society, in the period and place that you are studying, is largely of two kinds.

(i) Traders setting out, often in an extravagent manner, the goods or services they offer. Notice in Figure 8.2 the hours worked by the staff of the newspaper itself.

(ii) Private people setting out their 'wants'. These include both masters and mistresses requiring someone to undertake the multitude of jobs which society required; and servants in need of positions. For practical and legal reasons, organisations used local papers to issue statements of intent of various kinds. Meetings had to be publicised. The holding of auctions and other events required the presence of as many people as possible, and a widely read local paper is a good way of achieving this.

d) Letters

Every local newspaper prints its readers' views. For example, the *Birmingham Post*'s 1871 Christmas Day issue carries letters some of which might be written today. One is:

calling the attention of the proper authorities of Birmingham to the disgracefully dirty condition of our public thoroughfares ... there are certainly numbers of able-bodied men in Birmingham adapted for such work. Therefore why not employ them?

Another reader calls:

the attention of the police to the dangers arising from the game of "bandy" which is being daily carried on in the roads and streets. There is constant risk to passengers and windows from the stones thrown ... I see ... that the police force is ten men short of the regular number; perhaps this may account for the fact of my having sought a constable many times in vain, during the past fortnight, in this suburb.

('Bandy' was a kind of street hockey, played by opposing groups of children, who brandished sticks and rushed to and fro across the road in pursuit of a roughly rounded piece of wood!)

Fig. 8.2 The Birmingham Daily Post, 25th December 1871 edition, situations vacant etc.

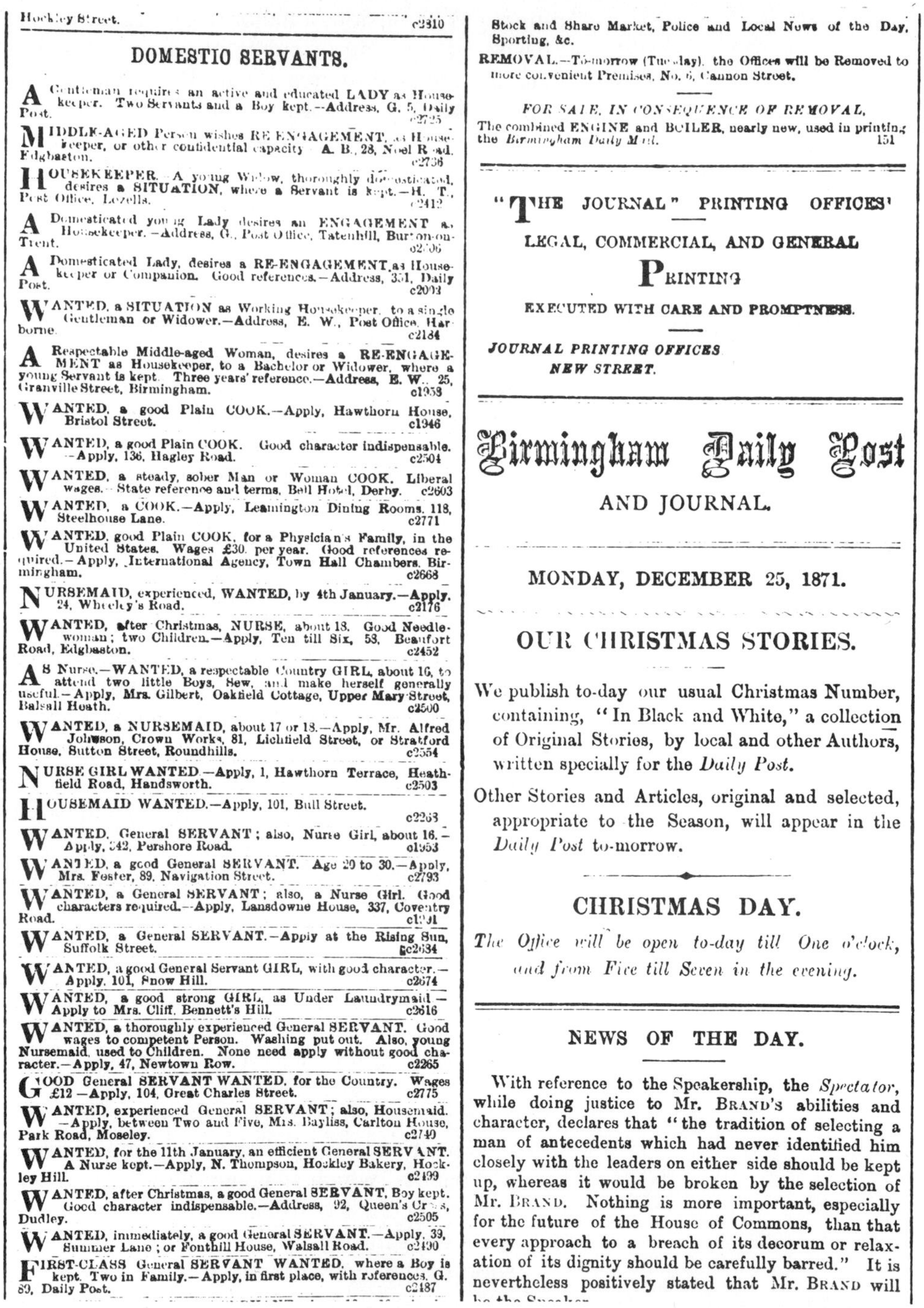

Hockley Street. c2310

DOMESTIC SERVANTS.

A Gentleman requires an active and educated LADY as Housekeeper. Two Servants and a Boy kept.--Address, G. 5, Daily Post. c2725

MIDDLE-AGED Person wishes RE-ENGAGEMENT, as Housekeeper, or other confidential capacity. A. B., 28, Noel Road, Edgbaston. c2736

HOUSEKEEPER.—A young Widow, thoroughly domesticated, desires a SITUATION, where a Servant is kept.—H. T., Post Office, Lozells. c2412

A Domesticated young Lady desires an ENGAGEMENT as Housekeeper.—Address, G., Post Office, Tatenhill, Burton-on-Trent. c2606

A Domesticated Lady, desires a RE-ENGAGEMENT as Housekeeper or Companion. Good references.—Address, 351, Daily Post. c2003

WANTED, a SITUATION as Working Housekeeper, to a single Gentleman or Widower.—Address, E. W., Post Office, Harborne. c2184

A Respectable Middle-aged Woman, desires a RE-ENGAGEMENT as Housekeeper, to a Bachelor or Widower, where a young Servant is kept. Three years' reference.—Address, E. W., 25, Granville Street, Birmingham. c1953

WANTED, a good Plain COOK.—Apply, Hawthorn House, Bristol Street. c1946

WANTED, a good Plain COOK. Good character indispensable. --Apply, 136, Hagley Road. c2504

WANTED, a steady, sober Man or Woman COOK. Liberal wages.—State reference and terms, Bell Hotel, Derby. c2603

WANTED, a COOK.—Apply, Leamington Dining Rooms, 118, Steelhouse Lane. c2771

WANTED, good Plain COOK, for a Physician's Family, in the United States. Wages £30. per year. Good references required.—Apply, International Agency, Town Hall Chambers, Birmingham. c2668

NURSEMAID, experienced, WANTED, by 4th January.—Apply, 24, Wheeley's Road. c2176

WANTED, after Christmas, NURSE, about 18. Good Needlewoman; two Children.—Apply, Ten till Six, 58, Beaufort Road, Edgbaston. c2452

AS Nurse.—WANTED, a respectable Country GIRL, about 16, to attend two little Boys, Sew, and make herself generally useful.—Apply, Mrs. Gilbert, Oakfield Cottage, Upper Mary Street, Balsall Heath. c2500

WANTED, a NURSEMAID, about 17 or 18.—Apply, Mr. Alfred Johnson, Crown Works, 81, Lichfield Street, or Stratford House, Sutton Street, Roundhills. c2554

NURSE GIRL WANTED.—Apply, 1, Hawthorn Terrace, Heathfield Road, Handsworth. c2503

HOUSEMAID WANTED.—Apply, 101, Bull Street. c2263

WANTED, General SERVANT; also, Nurse Girl, about 16.—Apply, 342, Pershore Road. c1953

WANTED, a good General SERVANT. Age 20 to 30.—Apply, Mrs. Foster, 89, Navigation Street. c2793

WANTED, a General SERVANT; also, a Nurse Girl. Good characters required.—Apply, Lansdowne House, 337, Coventry Road. c1991

WANTED, a General SERVANT.—Apply at the Rising Sun, Suffolk Street. c2634

WANTED, a good General Servant GIRL, with good character.—Apply, 101, Snow Hill. c2674

WANTED, a good strong GIRL, as Under Laundrymaid.—Apply to Mrs. Cliff, Bennett's Hill. c2616

WANTED, a thoroughly experienced General SERVANT. Good wages to competent Person. Washing put out. Also, young Nursemaid, used to Children. None need apply without good character.—Apply, 47, Newtown Row. c2265

GOOD General SERVANT WANTED, for the Country. Wages £12.—Apply, 104, Great Charles Street. c2775

WANTED, experienced General SERVANT; also, Housemaid. —Apply, between Two and Five, Mrs. Bayliss, Carlton House, Park Road, Moseley. c2740

WANTED, for the 11th January, an efficient General SERVANT. A Nurse kept.—Apply, N. Thompson, Hockley Bakery, Hockley Hill. c2499

WANTED, after Christmas, a good General SERVANT, Boy kept. Good character indispensable.—Address, 92, Queen's Cross, Dudley. c2505

WANTED, immediately, a good General SERVANT.—Apply, 39, Summer Lane; or Fonthill House, Walsall Road. c2490

FIRST-CLASS General SERVANT WANTED, where a Boy is kept. Two in Family.—Apply, in first place, with references, G. 89, Daily Post. c2487

Stock and Share Market, Police and Local News of the Day, Sporting, &c.

REMOVAL.—To-morrow (Tuesday), the Offices will be Removed to more convenient Premises, No. 6, Cannon Street.

FOR SALE, IN CONSEQUENCE OF REMOVAL,

The combined ENGINE and BOILER, nearly new, used in printing the *Birmingham Daily Mail.* 151

"THE JOURNAL" PRINTING OFFICES'

LEGAL, COMMERCIAL, AND GENERAL

PRINTING

EXECUTED WITH CARE AND PROMPTNESS.

JOURNAL PRINTING OFFICES
NEW STREET.

Birmingham Daily Post

AND JOURNAL.

MONDAY, DECEMBER 25, 1871.

OUR CHRISTMAS STORIES.

We publish to-day our usual Christmas Number, containing, "In Black and White," a collection of Original Stories, by local and other Authors, written specially for the *Daily Post.*

Other Stories and Articles, original and selected, appropriate to the Season, will appear in the *Daily Post* to-morrow.

CHRISTMAS DAY.

The Office will be open to-day till One o'clock, and from Five till Seven in the evening.

NEWS OF THE DAY.

With reference to the Speakership, the *Spectator,* while doing justice to Mr. BRAND'S abilities and character, declares that "the tradition of selecting a man of antecedents which had never identified him closely with the leaders on either side should be kept up, whereas it would be broken by the selection of Mr. BRAND. Nothing is more important, especially for the future of the House of Commons, than that every approach to a breach of its decorum or relaxation of its dignity should be carefully barred." It is nevertheless positively stated that Mr. BRAND will

WHERE?

Finding newspapers

Reference libraries and record offices hold many newspapers on microfilm, from which copies can be taken. Hard copies of the papers themselves are also held, but may not be accessible for research, especially if microfilm copies exist. Some local papers may have had an index made of its back issues.

If the local paper itself still exists, it will probably have microfilmed copies, and it may be worth making enquiries at their offices.

There are special collections of newspapers, which may well contain what you are seeking,* but be warned that access to them may not be as easy as going to your local library.

HSUs

Newspapers and the National Curriculum

The benefits are mainly for the study of Victorian and later periods. Newspapers are very important sources for the 1930s and the Second World War studies. Local studies will also benefit from local paper consultation.

ACTIVITIES

Using newspapers

1. Use a selection of advertisements from a local newspaper to find out about shops, prices, commodities etc. in your period.

2. Have a look at the advertisements in the *Birmingham Daily Post* (Figure 8.3), and in particular the section on Domestic Servants. Using evidence from several of these, build up a picture of what life must have been like for a housemaid or an errand boy.

3. Photocopy extracts from reports of cases in a Victorian magistrate's court and use them as evidence about crime and law enforcement in the 19th century.

4. Locate local coverage and textbook coverage of the same event (if possible several different papers and books). Ask children to compare the details, and draw up lists showing what is covered and in how much detail by which source. For example groups could investigate people by name and their details; dates; event details; etc. (This is an activity designed to exemplify Key Element 3 Interpretations of history.)

5. Choose a modern local event which parallels your area of study, and have the children each write a paragraph of newspaper report on it. (Perhaps the interview of a visitor about her experiences in the Second World War; or a visit to a local building or site). The point of this exercise is to emphasize the difference between different reporters, so children should write their

---

* The British Library national collection is held at Colindale, London NW6. A reader's pass is required to consult it. It is also essential to reserve a microfilm reader before going there; and before using such equipment, you must make sure that the library does actually hold papers for the place and period you require. This is done by using their eight-volume catalogue. You can ring to ask 'Have you local newspaper coverage of your place in such and such a date?' The Guildhall Library in London has a good 18th and 19th century collection. The Bodleian Library in Oxford also holds a strong collection. The National Libraries of Wales (Aberystwyth) and Scotland (Edinburgh) house their national collections.

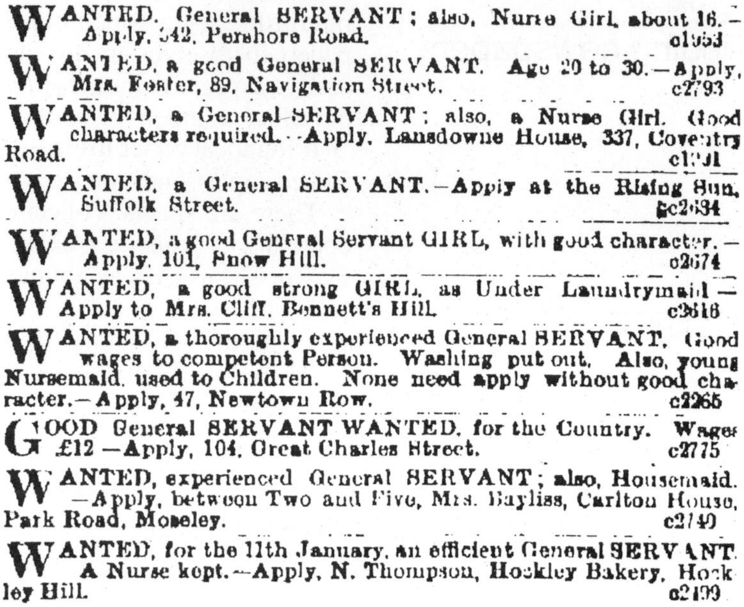

WANTED. General SERVANT; also, Nurse Girl about 16. –
Apply, 342, Pershore Road.   c1953

WANTED, a good General SERVANT.   Age 20 to 30. – Apply,
Mrs. Foster, 89, Navigation Street.   c2793

WANTED, a General SERVANT; also, a Nurse Girl. Good
characters required. – Apply, Lansdowne House, 337, Coventry
Road.   c1791

WANTED, a General SERVANT. – Apply at the Rising Sun,
Suffolk Street.   c2634

WANTED, a good General Servant GIRL, with good character. –
Apply, 101, Snow Hill.   c2674

WANTED, a good strong GIRL, as Under Laundrymaid –
Apply to Mrs. Cliff, Bennett's Hill.   c3618

WANTED, a thoroughly experienced General SERVANT. Good
wages to competent Person. Washing put out. Also, young
Nursemaid, used to Children. None need apply without good character. – Apply, 47, Newtown Row.   c2265

GOOD General SERVANT WANTED, for the Country. Wages
£12 – Apply, 104, Great Charles Street.   c2775

WANTED, experienced General SERVANT; also, Housemaid.
– Apply, between Two and Five, Mrs. Bayliss, Carlton House,
Park Road, Moseley.   c2740

WANTED, for the 11th January, an efficient General SERVANT.
A Nurse kept. – Apply, N. Thompson, Hockley Bakery, Hockley Hill.   c2199

Fig 8.3 *A selection from*
Figure 8.2

reports separately. In presenting the results to the class, these differences should be stressed as highlighting the way we look at historic reports.

6. Answer one of the advertisements illustrated.

7. If you have access to a whole newspaper from the past, or a recognisable whole page (the front page, the sports page, etc.), compare it with today's equivalent. Get the children to discuss in groups how they differ. Among the differences to look out for might be:

❒ the use of illustrations

❒ the use of good English

❒ spelling mistakes

❒ the style of writing particular kinds of piece (compare sports reports, for instance)

❒ prices

❒ the kinds of job that are advertised

❒ the kinds of goods and services advertised

❒ the kind of people who would read the paper.

PROBLEMS
Possible difficulties using newspapers

The greatest problem, undoubtedly, is finding a local paper which covers your place in your period. You may be able to call on a neighbouring publication (the paper covering the neighbouring town is still more interesting than that of a remote place). We can only wish you luck in this respect!

Bias in the report is of great importance. Bear in mind the politics of the event described and the kind of person being reported. (Will the reporting of a strike be reported in the same way as an annual meeting of the Poor Law Commissioners?) What coverage is given to the weddings of the upper, middle and working classes? Do not overlook the kind of person likely to be doing the reporting; and think about the kind of people he was writing for (the reporter was likely to have been a man!).

Errors in the reporting are not easy to check. But it is worth bearing in mind how often reporters make mistakes in today's newspapers, such as wrong ages given, relationships between people not correctly stated, past history not reported correctly. The latter is a particularly rich area for potential mistakes: if the reporter says 'She was attacked in the same woods two years ago too', who told him this? Probably the girl herself; but did she remember the date correctly?

All these problems help to illustrate the shortcomings of some historical sources as evidence today.

9 Oral history

BACKGROUND

The importance of oral history

Oral history simply means the spoken accounts of events and experiences in the past by those present at the time. They have always been a part of history, but the invention of the tape recorder has made this kind of history much easier to collect and to communicate to others, and there is now a much wider acceptance of the importance of personal accounts.

For obvious reasons, oral history tends to concentrate on the comparatively recent past, although some people born in Victorian times have been recorded. (In 1940 the BBC recorded a man who as a boy had witnessed the funeral of the Duke of Wellington). Oral history has also proved to be a good way of finding out about the personal experiences of working people, women and minority groups who might not otherwise get into the history books. The spoken word has an immediacy lacking in most books, perhaps because it tends to be less balanced and carefully considered than written text, but this also means that it must be assessed cautiously.

WHERE?

Finding oral history recordings

A number of museums and sound archives like the National Sound Archive in London, Bradford Heritage Recording Unit, the North West Sound Archive and Leicester Oral History Archive have published oral history selections, often with a combination of tapes and printed extracts and sometimes photographs or slides. Unpublished recordings are also held by many other museums, and you should contact your own local museum or local studies library to find out what is available. You may find that they hold tapes of broadcasts by the local radio station which, if they have been indexed, can be a good source of material. They may also be able to give advice about equipment and techniques if you are going to get your children involved in interviewing older people, (especially if you offer them copies of the tapes).

HSUs

Oral history and the National Curriculum

At KS1, the orders specifically mention eyewitness accounts and "adults talking about their own past", and it is obvious that oral sources will have an advantage over written ones at this age.

At KS2, oral history has a vital contribution to make in SU3b *Britain Since 1930* and can contribute to any Local History Unit which extends into the 20th century.

At KS3 there will be valuable opportunities to use oral history when studying such topics as the changing status of women in *The 20th Century World*.

Using oral history

There are basically two ways of using oral history in school: by using existing tapes and transcripts, or by involving children in making their own recordings. These can become a real contribution to historical knowledge if copies are deposited in an appropriate local archive, but it does take careful planning and a little practice to achieve recordings that will be useful to other people. This is also an activity which brings older people into contact with children in school and can have social benefits as well as historical ones.

Using existing recordings

The advantage of using published oral selections or unpublished tapes from a local archive is that children have access to professionally produced material from a wide range of interviews. Subjects like transport, school, childhood, the experience of immigrant workers, clothes, entertainment and many others can be brought to life by oral evidence. Teachers may need to select from the original interviews extracts which are relevant to the children's work at this time, so that they are not overwhelmed by a mass of information on different aspects of the subject or bored by long recordings. Oral history should always be seen as part of the picture and used alongside other types of evidence.

Doing your own interviews

Getting children to carry out their own interviews may mean restricting the study to a very small sample (perhaps only one person), but it has the great merit of involving them directly in real research through which they can develop important historical skills.

It is sometimes possible to arrange for more than one person to be interviewed, either in a series of class sessions or by different small groups of three or four children. (Communicating their findings to the rest of the class is another valuable learning experience linking with other parts of the curriculum.) The value of this approach is that different answers to the same questions can be compared and assessed, and a wider range of information added to the investigation. The comparison of different accounts of the past, and recognising the difference between fact and opinion are essential historical skills.

Preparing for an interview

Talk to the person who is going to be interviewed and make sure they know what sort of things the children are likely to ask about. Explain what the children have been doing and how the interview is going to be conducted, and generally help them to feel at ease, especially if they are not used to visiting the school.

Before children attempt an interview they will need to practise the techniques in class, perhaps with the teacher acting as the person being interviewed. This will help to develop confidence and highlight potential problems or approaches which work well. They should notice the kinds of question that encourage interesting answers: "What did you think?", "What did it feel like?" rather than "Did you like it?", which is likely to bring simply a "Yes" or "No" reply.

A list of questions should be prepared beforehand, and it is an essential part of the exercise that children should be involved in drawing up the list. However, there can be a tendency for them then to rush through such a list, ticking off each question when it has been "done", but paying little attention to the answers. One strategy is to encourage them to go back over those items on the list where they thought the person had more to tell them. The aim is to think of the interview as a conversation on a number of topic areas, rather than having too many specific questions to get through. After an interview it is a good idea to get children to write down what they found most interesting, so that they are encouraged to sort out important points from the mass of topics covered.

The use of old photographs or even picture books is a good way of highlighting important points with young children. They use the pictures as prompts both for themselves and for the interviewee, selecting things in the pictures they would like to know more about. In the same way, artefacts or old newspapers can be used both as a stimulus for memories and as a way of comparing different sources of information.

Exploring the history of your school

The school itself can be the stimulus for older people to talk about what it was like to go to school when they were children. Rather than sitting in one classroom, let the children take their subject around several rooms, into the main hall to talk about dinners and assemblies, to the playground for the games and memories of friends they played with. Oral history works well when looking at education since 1930, complementing other sources such as log books and old photographs, and, because children have experience of the context, they can devise their own investigations and ask their own questions.

Other topics

Teachers will have no difficulty thinking of other topics that can be investigated using oral history. Many aspects of life since 1930 can be made more real through the detail that older people's memories will often be able to supply.

Clothes, games, entertainments, housework, warwork, rationing, holidays, shops and travel are just a few. It is people's feelings about things, as much as events at which they were present, that are the unique contribution of this kind of history. Remember that oral accounts should always be used in conjunction with other types of evidence.

Whether to record

Oral history does not have to be recorded on tape, but it is much more useful if it is. A recording allows the interview to be re-examined and details checked at a later date, and of course it means that it can be shared with others not present at the time, including next year's class. Copies should always be offered to your local museum or sound archive.

Possible difficulties with interviewing

It is very important to choose the right kind of person to be interviewed: someone who is going to be sympathetic to the children and help build their confidence as well as knowing the answers to their questions.

Poor or faulty equipment can ruin a good interview. Tape recorders do not have to be very expensive, sophisticated models, but they should be working satisfactorily. (Check the batteries!) A small clip-on lapel microphone is best, but a built-in microphone in the recorder may be better than a large and intrusive one placed intimidatingly in front of the interviewee.

10 Parish registers

BACKGROUND
Development of parish registers

As a way of keeping track of the nation's population, Henry VIII's government required all Anglican priests to keep lists of births, marriages and deaths. These were to be stored in specially acquired, lockable chests. The Act (1538) did not specify how the records were to be kept, and it was 60 years before a bound book was required.

At first, entries were recorded together, on sheets of paper, parchment, etc, in whatever order they happened. Gradually, however, different registers were used for each event.

The information recorded on the early documents, and in the first books, varied. The data were only as good as the enthusiasm, literary ability and handwriting of the recorders concerned. Not until 1711 did another act specify that a proper register, with ruled and numbered pages should be used.

The earliest Roman Catholic registers date from the mid 16th century.

The Act of 1598 also required the churchwardens to make a copy of the main register, once a year, to send to their bishop. These 'Bishop's Transcripts' are specially useful when the original registers are lost, damaged or illegible. They are also a cross-check on the spelling of names and on dates.

The Civil War, with the rise in puritanism, and foundation of many nonconformist religious sects, led to many Anglican and Catholic registers being suppressed. In some parishes there are no records at all until after the Restoration; in others there are gaps during the Interregnum. The Cromwellian government did make provision for the registration of births, marriages and deaths, but only a few of these registers survive.

From the mid 17th century (but mainly from the 18th and early 19th centuries), the registers survive of various nonconformist sects; and of the Jewish religion.

By the middle 1700s, a number of irregularities had developed in marriage practices. Priests who were in prison for debt were marrying couples while in gaol ('Fleet marriages'); some rectors and vicars* had become lax about who they would marry. Thus some would, for a fee, marry couples who already had children; the widowed (other priests would not); the under-aged; and so on.

---

* The difference between these titles relates to the tithes they received. A rector was entitled by right (Latin *recto*) to collect tithes. However, many of these rights had been appropriated by religious orders or lay men and women. In these cases, religious duties were performed by a vicar (Latin *vicarius*, a substitute). Then the Rectorial tithes – the main benefits of corn, hay, wood etc, which were easiest to collect – were kept by the institution or lay person. This left the vicar to collect the lesser tithes (minor produce and labour).

Also, some alternative places were used for weddings, principally the blacksmith at Gretna Green.

In 1754, to tighten up marriage practices and recording generally, a new act outlawed these 'irregular' marriages. It also made provision for the recording of banns; and a number of the resulting Banns registers survive.

What do the records tell us?

In the fictitious examples below, the entries are designed to show the legal minimum that registers should have given. Not all registers gave all the information; a few added extra wording, giving tantalising glimpses into the past.

Baptism records

Originally these gave only the simplest facts:

17 May 1605 *Margaret Ross baptised*

Fig. 10.1 *Marriage register entry for 18th April 1797, St Chad, Wybunbury, Cheshire*

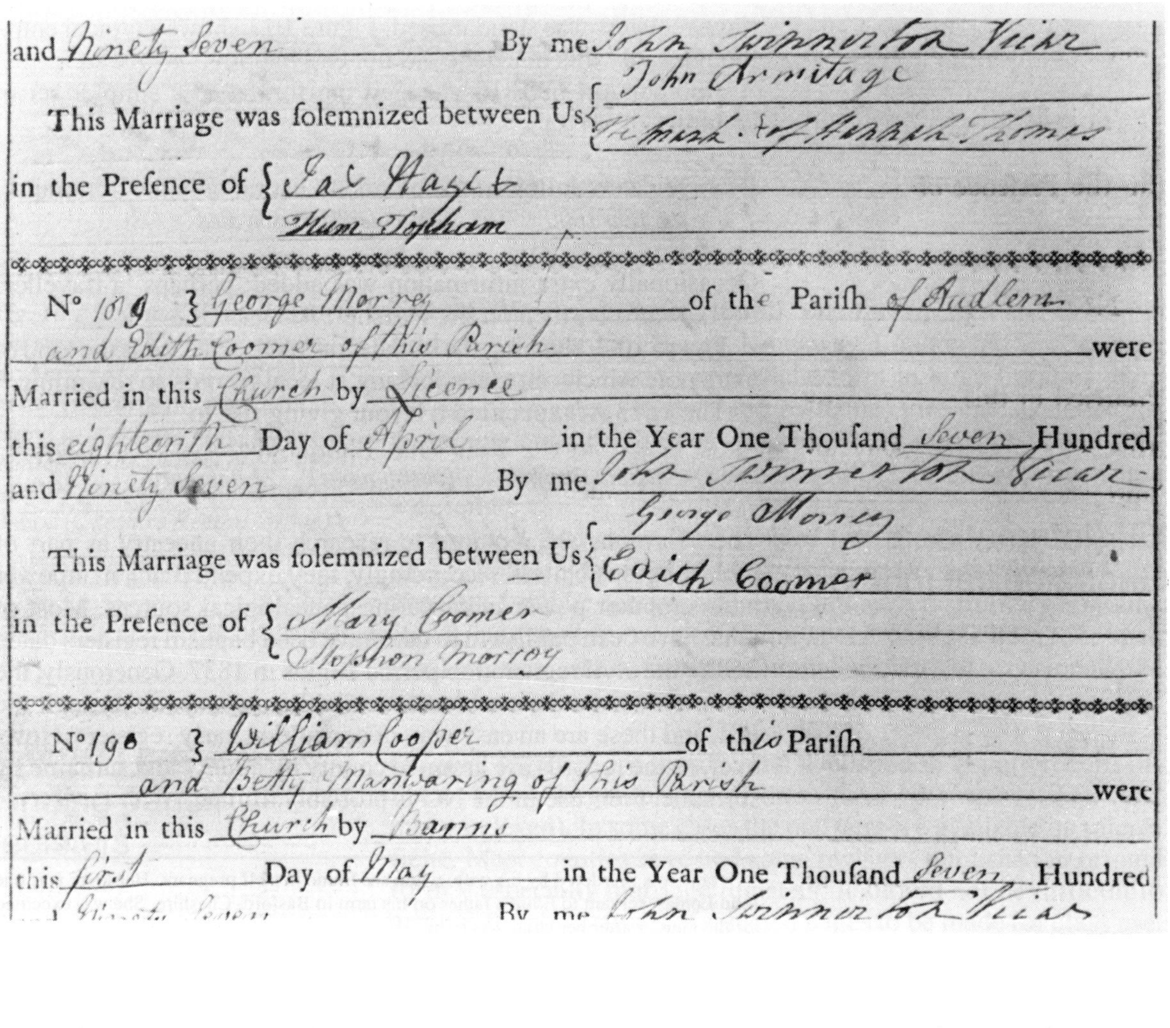

and Ninety Seven By me John Swinnerton Vicar

This Marriage was ſolemnized between Us { John Armitage / The mark + of Hannah Thomas

in the Preſence of { Jac Hazlet / Hum Topham

N° 189 } George Morrey of the Pariſh of Audlem and Edith Coomer of this Parish were Married in this Church by Licence this eighteenth Day of April in the Year One Thouſand Seven Hundred and Ninety Seven By me John Swinnerton Vicar

This Marriage was ſolemnized between Us { George Morrey / Edith Coomer

in the Preſence of { Mary Coomer / Stephen Morrey

N° 190 } William Cooper of this Pariſh and Betty Manwaring of this Parish were Married in this Church by Banns this first Day of May in the Year One Thouſand Seven Hundred and Ninety Seven By me John Swinnerton Vicar

Reference libraries and specialist museums are also places to seek the registers of particular groups of people.

Modern registers are not accessible for research in libraries; they remain in the church or chapel concerned.

HSUs

Parish registers and the National Curriculum

At KS1 parish registers might be used to look at the forenames and surnames which were popular, to make comparisons with those in use today.

Parish registers are likely to be most helpful in the 16th to 18th centuries, although the number of useful ones accessible is small in the 16th century.

Consequently, SU2 *Life in Tudor Times* and the Local History Unit are ones most likely to benefit from the use of parish registers. General information about birth and death rates based on local registers could illustrate national trends, or a particular local family could be studied in detail.

At KS3 it will again be evidence about births and deaths which will be relevant to a study of health and disease in the Unit on *Britain 1750–c1900*.

ACTIVITIES

Using parish registers

Most of the following activities could be conducted using two sequences each of roughly the same number of baptisms, marriages and deaths, (not less than 50 each), taken from the same periods 100 years or so apart (for example births marriages and deaths from 1600 to about 1625; and the same registers from 1700 to about 1725). If you can locate the registers for the second half of the 19th century, samples from this period can usefully be compared with censuses and directories.

1. Look at all the registers. Can you identify the same families in all three registers? What can you find out about them? (Build up family trees).

2. Check the 100-year-apart sample to see how mobile people were. (A surprisingly low percentage of surnames from the earlier period will still be present a hundred years later).

3. Look at all the registers and note the number of births of boys and girls; the ages of burials (were more children buried than adults?); the ages of adults at death. Did men or women die younger on average?

4. Analyse each register sample, using IT and present the results as graphs/pie-charts/etc, to see whether there are changes in the numbers of births, marriages and deaths between the two periods. Have the proportions of births:marriages:deaths changed? (Are there more births per marriage, for instance?) Can you think why any changes might have happened?

5. Using the burials register sample covering your period, is there any evidence for epidemics? If this looks likely, and if you can use any other source to pinpoint where people lived (census/

poll register/directory), plot the deaths on to a map.

6. Check the burials register for any evidence of travellers dying while passing through your area. Where might they have been going to?

7. Check the marriage register to see how far grooms travelled to find their brides; and whether on occasions both bride and groom travelled to your parish to get married. Plot what you find on to a map of your locality (i.e. your parish and those surrounding it), and see if you can discover how far people travelled: perhaps even why.

8. Try and find out about (perhaps even make contact with decendants of) a group of people getting married in your period. Put on a display of the results of your enquiries.

9. Are all the registers evenly distributed in their periods? Are there periods when baptisms are few, followed by periods when many are entered at the same time? Can you think why?

Handling data from parish registers

IT

The investigation of parish registers provides another opportunity for the use of data handling applications. They can be used in a similar way to census returns and can help children achieve an understanding of local history over a longer period of time than is possible with census returns, albeit with less detail.

A datafile of parish registers might consist of simply the MONTH, YEAR, NAME and EVENT (i.e. Baptised, Married, Buried). Even very young children can create such a datafile relatively easily. Some data handling programs allow the teacher to create a list of choices from which children can select when entering the data, thus helping to reduce the incidence of typing errors. Children can then analyse the numbers of baptisms, marriages and deaths over a reasonable period, looking for particularly significant incidents (such as an epidemic) or identify events occurring more frequently in some months than in others. Clearly, the larger the sample of data, the more meaningful the analysis will be, and several hundred records would probably be a reasonable minimum to aim at over time. Graphs can be produced which illustrate particular aspects of the data very quickly and easily.

Spreadsheets

Parish registers can also conveniently be analysed using spreadsheets in a similar way. A spreadsheet is rather like a two-dimensional calculator; it consists of a collection of information in the form of numbers or words (see Figure 10.3), which can be manipulated, tabulated and graphed. Children can set up a spreadsheet and then use it to carry out calculations. Thus, for example, the average number of baptisms, marriages or burials for each month over a number of years, can be compared with the details for a specific year very quickly and easily. Spreadsheets can also often produce more sophisticated graphical displays of the data than are possible with straightforward data handling

	JAN	FEB	MAR	APR	MAY	JUN	JUL	AUG	SEP	OCT	NOV	DEC	Total
1601	0	0	1	5	1	1	2	1	1	2	0	1	15
1602	1	0	1	3	0	2	3	1	0	5	1	3	20
1603	4	0	2	1	15	1	2	2	1	2	0	2	32
1604	3	2	6	1	2	2	2	4	4	1	3	3	33
1605	0	2	0	2	1	1	2	4	3	2	1	2	20
1606	1	5	2	2	3	1	0	1	2	1	4	4	26
1607	0	3	3	2	4	3	1	2	0	3	0	4	25
1608	4	1	2	1	3	4	3	2	0	0	0	7	27
1609	3	0	3	0	0	1	1	1	1	4	1	1	16
1610	0	5	1	2	3	1	1	2	0	0	0	1	16
1611	0	1	1	0	0	0	0	0	0	0	0	0	2
1612	1	2	2	2	3	2	2	2	1	2	1	2	22
1613	1	2	0	0	0	0	2	1	1	1	0	0	8
1614	0	0	1	1	1	2	1	2	0	1	0	2	11
1615	0	2	2	1	2	6	1	1	0	1	2	1	19
1616	1	2	2	7	9	10	0	0	3	3	3	3	43
1617	1	2	3	0	1	4	2	4	3	2	0	0	22
1618	5	4	2	5	4	2	3	1	1	1	4	0	32
1619	1	1	6	2	4	2	2	0	1	4	2	3	28
1620	1	2	2	2	3	2	3	2	1	1	3	1	23
Mean	1.43	1.80	2.00	1.80	2.57	2.20	1.80	1.63	1.20	1.70	1.27	2.33	21.73

Fig. 10.3

applications, thus allowing more detailed analysis and investigation.

A spreadsheet of details from parish registers is probably best produced using a summary of the information extracted for each month in each year. Thus, for the analysis of burials over a period of time, a spreadsheet might be set up similar to the example in Figure 10.3. The spreadsheet calculates the total for each year, as well as the mean number of burials for each month and for the total. This information can then be graphed to compare any number of specific years with the mean; or to identify whether more burials occurred in some months than others; or, if a suitably large number of entries is available, whether particular incidents (such as war, famine or epidemics) are reflected in the local statistics.

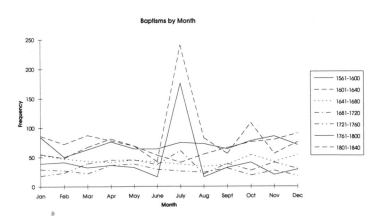

*Fig. 10.4 Baptism by months
1561-1840*

Marriages and baptisms can be analysed in a similar way and graphed (Figure 10.4), to see, perhaps, whether more baptisms or marriages occurred in some months than others; or on which days of the week marriages and baptisms took place. It's always fun to speculate why some months have more baptisms than others, and marriages often took take place on other days than Saturdays in the past.

PROBLEMS

Possible difficulties using parish registers
Gaps

For various reasons registers are not always complete. Apart from years when apparently no baptisms, marriages or burials took place, there may be periods during a year when fewer events were recorded than usual. Registers may be affected by epidemics, for example. Records in Beverley, North Humberside, for 1610 show that so many parishioners died in the month of August in that year that no entries at all were made in the registers. Gaps often occur during the Civil War period.

These are issues for children to consider when thinking about the reliability of historical evidence.

Dates

Remember that the calendar changed in 1752. Up to that year, New Year's day was 25 March. Dates in January and February in the years before 1752 are sometimes (today) expressed as, say 1750/51. Also, eleven days were removed from the calendar during September 1752. No one could have been baptised, married or buried, for example, on 10 September!

Handwriting

In most cases, the class will be working from transcripts, though it is useful for children to see what the real thing looked like. Registers were written by clerics who were, of course, literate; but naturally their handwriting varied in quality. The handwriting used in the 16th and 17th centuries takes a little getting used to. Your library will have useful guides if you wish to 'translate' register sequences for class use.

Latin

During the Neoclassical period (1700-1825, say), many registers used Latin forms of 'ordinary' English Christian names (Henricus/Jacobus/etc.).

Abbreviations

Especially during this Latinised period, some abbreviations one may meet are not immediately obvious (e.g. 's' = *sepultus* = buried).

11 Photographs and pictures

Development of photography

Photography dates back to 1839 when a wealthy gentleman, William Henry Fox Talbot of Lacock Abbey in Somerset, announced his invention of the "calotype" process. Only shortly before this a Frenchman, Daguerre, had invented his own method called "Daguerrotypes", but it was the Fox Talbot system based on the use of negatives which was the forerunner of modern photography.

It was at first an expensive, and for most of the 19th century a laborious business, involving cumbersome equipment both for exposing the glass plate negatives and for developing and printing the images. Shutter speeds were slow and any people in the picture had to be rigidly posed, sometimes even with the help of a wooden brace attached to the back of the studio chair. Not until the invention of roll film and the easily portable box camera right at the end of the century did photography become a popular pastime.

Photographs, however, were popular right from the start, and were taken and sold by an increasing number of professional

Fig. 11.1 Boulter's Lock, Maidenhead, Berkshire, 1890. Evidence about leisure, clothes (especially hats), and the roles of men and women

photographers up and down the country specialising in studio portraits, cartes de visite, and picturesque views of places which sold as picture postcards. There was also a great interest in lectures illustrated with glass lantern slides, one of the first and most enduring educational visual aids. Highly gifted men as well as many others with less skill but great energy photographed everything from soldiers in the Crimea to children's May Day processions; from Queen Victoria at the Crystal Palace to the humblest labourer's cottage.

The expansion of popular photography in this century is well known. The still photograph, let alone the moving image, has become an essential part of everyday life and the whole century has been thoroughly recorded in this way. Among the millions that have survived from the past 150 years there will be plenty to support a local study or to provide local evidence for national history, but like all evidence they need to be assessed critically.

The same is more obviously true of other kinds of picture – water-colour paintings and drawings reproduced by one or other of the several printing processes available. It was a long time before a satisfactory method of printing photographs onto newsprint was invented and in the 1880s elaborate pictures like those in the *Illustrated London News* were still produced by hand-engraving the images captured in photographs onto boxwood blocks, and fastening several together to make large spreads. Apart from news pictures like these (many of which report events outside London), most towns and some smaller places will have prints and drawings perhaps going back as far as the 18th century.

Where?
Finding photographs and pictures

Old prints and drawings will be found in your local archive office or local studies library and in many local museums. It is also worth searching for published copies in local history books about your area (but remember the copyright law which restricts the further copies you can make from this source).

In most parts of the country you should also find large collections of old photographs in the same places. Some of these collections are very large, consisting of over 100,000 images. The extent to which they are catalogued will vary. They are most likely to be listed under places, but they may also list topics such as "vehicles", "children", "crafts", etc. although for obvious reasons it is difficult to classify everything which appears in a photograph. Again, many books of old photographs and local postcard views of towns and villages all over the country have been published. Some of these will already have selected 'then and now' pictures, which nicely illustrate change and continuity.

Photocopies of photographs are not very satisfactory unless done on a "laser" copier, in which case very good results can be achieved quite cheaply. Otherwise it is a matter of paying to have photographic prints made, and most offices and libraries offer this service.

HSUs

Photographs, pictures and the National Curriculum

ACTIVITIES

Using photographs and pictures
Assessing photographs as historical evidence

It will be obvious to teachers that pictorial sources can be used to support the local history elements of the National Curriculum at all Key Stages, especially at KS1 where young children will find them easier than written sources.

Like other kinds of unofficial documentation they raise issues of bias and interpretation.

The camera records accurately what is in front of the lens, but it is the photographer who decides what that should be and how it should be arranged. What might at first appear to be a fortunate or skilful capturing of the fleeting moment – the girl drawing water from a stream or a group of children in their May procession – may in fact be a carefully posed shot. The solemn, almost grim expressions on the faces of children in school group photographs tell us something about the atmosphere and discipline in Victorian schools, but are also partly the result of the need to keep absolutely still while the photograph was being taken. Such photographs have a considerable value as historical evidence, but the circumstances in which they were taken and the purpose for which they were intended should always be considered. This applies even to topographical pictures where the appearance of buildings cannot be changed but the atmosphere of the scene is affected by the people in it. Is the village street so deserted because that was its normal state or because the photographer wanted to avoid movement which would blur in the slow exposure? Alternatively, are the groups of people carefully posed to achieve a picturesque effect?

When using a photograph, children should be encouraged to ask "Why was this picture taken? How was it taken?" and "Is it likely to be a posed or a natural shot?"

Sequencing

Putting a group of photographs into chronological order using clues within the pictures – styles of clothing, horsedrawn or motor vehicles, furniture, gas lighting, etc. – is a valuable exercise and fun as well. It teaches very young children at KS1 the concept of change, and it can be a more sophisticated exercise of historical skills with older children, applying their knowledge of the past (e.g. when cars were invented or when people wore "bustles") to date the photograph.

"Then and Now" – observing change and continuity

An extension of the sequencing exercise is to examine two or more pictures of the same local scene and to explore them for evidence of change. Examples might be two photographs of the school at different dates, or two local street scenes with people, vehicles and shopfronts. In large towns there will often be old prints or paintings showing the main streets, allowing the sequence to be extended back before photography. The final stage in this process is to take a modern photograph of the same view today, involving the children in this if practical. The interest lies not only in what has changed but also in what has stayed the same, and in why these things have happened and the effect on people's lives.

Fig. 11.2 Broadway,
Worcestershire, 1900

Fig. 11.3 Broadway,
Worcestershire, 1993

Taking photographs

As well as using old photographs and pictures, children can use photography themselves to record the places or individual buildings they have been studying. A photograph is a good way of concentrating attention on particular features of interest, and better than laborious and inaccurate drawings. Photographs are also an effective way for children to present their findings and to communicate them to others, itself an important part of the historical process.

| IT |

Using a concept keyboard with photographs and pictures

The use of local photographs and pictures provides another opportunity for children to use a concept keyboard in a way similar to that described earlier in Chapter 7, Maps and Air Photographs. Children can use a concept keyboard with a range of other sources to investigate local history in an exciting and highly motivating way.

As described previously, a concept keyboard provides an alternative means of communicating with the computer. By pressing the touch sensitive surface over which has been placed a photograph or picture, children can be given information, asked questions or set additional tasks. Use of the concept keyboard with pictures and photographs can provide a highly motivating stimulus for the investigation of other sources and can genuinely make those sources more easily accessible to children.

Concept keyboard software allows teachers to create an overlay; some programs such as Touch Explorer Plus can contain several layers of information for each square on the concept keyboard.

Fig. 11.4 Lithograph of Chipping Norton, Oxfordshire, market place, 1861. Successfully used as an overlay for investigation with the concept keyboard

Relating these levels to tasks which require additional research from amongst the additional sources provides perhaps the most exciting opportunities for children. Using sources to answer a specific question or to carry out a "real" task can make the sources more accessible, and can lead to a greater understanding of the source concerned. The teacher might provide copies of census returns related to the inhabitants of buildings in a picture or photograph, and children could be asked to investigate the census returns to find the family concerned. They might be asked to list the members of the family, to find their ages and occupations, whether they had servants, where they were born, etc. Relevant local contemporary newspaper extracts and commercial directories can provide additional information which children can research.

Creating a concept keyboard overlay is straightforward and will be described in detail in the program documentation. Collecting source material relating to the picture or photograph can be a little time consuming but is well worth the effort. The key to the successful creation of a concept keyboard overlay is careful planning and organisation on the teacher's part. The information, questions and additional tasks children will be given when they press the picture or photograph should be planned and organised, before one begins creating the concept keyboard overlay. Once these issues have been decided, typing the information into the computer is a relatively quick and straightforward concern.

If children are to gain as much as possible from the use of a concept keyboard picture or photograph and source materials, there are certain considerations to bear in mind. First, they must be introduced to the source material available and they should understand how and why the evidence was originally collected and what information they are likely to find in each source. To gain as much as possible they must be able to use sources confidently and efficiently.

Secondly, it is clear that any picture or photograph and its associated source material can contain a wealth of information, questions and additional activities. No one group of children will have time to complete an "exploration" of the entire picture through all its levels. It may be necessary for teachers to allocate a period of time for each group of children to "explore" the picture with time away from the computer to complete the tasks and activities suggested during the course of their exploration. It is important, however, that children have the chance to share the results of their investigations with one another and the rest of the class.

Thirdly, children will enjoy exploring history in this way. It is important that children's investigations are given some focus, however, and that they are encouraged to write about their discoveries and conclusions. Children can be encouraged take a particular theme as the focus for their investigation, such as transport and travel, occupations, clothing, and so on. They might be encouraged to produce a newspaper, diary, postcard etc., or they might make some comparisons between then and now. In this way children can combine the results of their investigations with additional research about their particular theme.

One considerable advantage of the use of the concept keyboard with pictures or photographs and original source materials is that children need to carry out real research, the results of which need to be assimilated and communicated. By using real sources about real people children can gain a considerably greater understanding of the topic or issue under investigation.

PROBLEMS
Quality of photographs and pictures

The only problem likely to be encountered may be that of obtaining good quality copies for classroom use. Poor photocopies obscure much of the detail and are therefore unsatisfactory. If "laser" copies are not available, it is worth spending the additional money to get a few well chosen photographic prints.

12 School log books

Development of school log books

Concern about the rising cost of expenditure on elementary education in the mid 19th century, and a not unfamiliar desire on the part of central government to make local schools more efficient both in their use of public funds and in their delivery of a basic core curriculum consisting of the "3 Rs", led to the introduction of the Revised Code of 1862. Among other things, this laid down that every school in receipt of government grant must keep a record of its day-to-day activities.

> The Principal Teacher must daily make in the Log Book the briefest entry which will suffice to specify either ordinary progress, or whatever other fact concerning the School or its Teachers, such as the dates of withdrawals, commencement of duty, cautions, illness, &c, may require to be referred to at a future time, or may otherwise deserve to be recorded. No reflections or opinions of a general character are to be entered in the Log Book.

In spite of this rather severe injunction, there is a wealth of interesting detail (and some revealing comment) to be found in surviving school log books. They form part of the school's own archive, which may also include managers' minutes, accounts, correspondence with one of the voluntary societies, registers and punishment books. They probably tell us more than any other record about the experience of going to school in the 19th century and earlier part of this century.

Finding school log books

Not all schools have old log books. The school itself may not be very old, or old log books which once existed may have been lost or even destroyed. It is a sad fact that schools have not always recognised their value or looked after them as carefully as they should have done.

Old log books should be in the local archive office and this is where many can be found. Most county archives hold over a hundred volumes, so there will be no problem in finding local examples even if the ones for your own school do not exist. Although they may be used in the record office, it is not always possible to obtain photocopies of pages because of restrictions on copying any bound volume which could be damaged in the process of pressing it flat on the copier. This means either using log books in the record office (check what facilities are available for schools), copying short extracts by hand, or using published extracts from other log books.

If your school still has its old log books, the correct thing to do is to deposit them in the record office, but arrange to have parts of it copied first for use in school.

In some repositories (e.g. the Centre for Oxfordshire Studies) all log books have been copied onto microfiche, and pages can be printed from this.

HSUs
School log books and the National Curriculum

Because of their specific nature, the range of uses of log books in the history curriculum is going to be limited, but they are very important sources in those parts where they are relevant. This will be mainly at KS2 in the *Victorian Britain* Unit or in a local study of education.

Quite apart from the content, they are examples of handwriting. Did the Victorian headteachers who taught their pupils copperplate practise it themselves?

ACTIVITIES
Using school log books

The use of log books is straightforward. They are a source of first-hand information about school life in the past, and investigating them is a very good way for children to develop skills of historical inquiry in a context which is within their own experience. Topics on which they will provide information usually include the following.

❑ Lessons taught (and sometimes the timetable)

❑ Annual inspection and testing of children by HMI.

❑ Summaries of the HMI reports

❑ Purchases of new equipment, books and furniture

❑ Names of teachers, pupil teachers and sometimes monitors

❑ Punishments

❑ Attendance figures and reasons for absence.

As usual with local sources, one or two extracts can be used to illustrate information gathered from books, or several pages can be used by children to investigate selected topics. These might be "What lessons were being taught?" or "Why did children sometimes stay away from school?"

Reasons for absence

This is a particularly fruitful inquiry because it will throw light on several aspects of domestic life such as low wages, child labour, sickness and the effect of weather and the farming cycle on rural life. It could also lead to discussion about the attitudes of different people – parents, children, teachers, employers – to attendance at school, thus fitting the study of a local school into a wider social context. Extracts like the following could be used:

> Several children are irregular. William Wright is employed by Mr. Hemstock as errand boy. He attends 5 and 6 times a week, has been warned from the Board Office, but apparently with little or no effect. He receives 1/- per week and his food, which is a great relief to his

parents with a large family. The boy is in Second Standard and will not be able to pass.

The facts of the case are pretty straightforward, but the background could be explored further. What was the work of an errand boy? It was a very common occupation for boys in the 19th century. How old was William Wright? How much was 1/- worth in the 1870s? If this was a small community it might be possible to find the Wright family in the census returns and to find out how large it was and what the parents' occupations were. It may also be possible to find Mr. Hemstock in the census or in a commercial directory. Finally, children could use roleplay to consider the standpoints of Mr. Hemstock, the members of the Board, the Wright parents and William Wright himself.

Almost any aspect of school life can be illustrated or investigated through log books, and they will repay the time spent by teachers in selecting extracts for children to use. This is necessary, as with most documentary sources at this level, in order to make the task manageable for children.

PROBLEMS

Possible difficulties using school logs

The most likely problem will be in obtaining copies for classroom use as mentioned above, but a lot of useful work can be based on quite short extracts copied by hand if no other method is available.

The emphasis in this chapter has been on using log books to study school in the Victorian period. They can also carry the study into the 20th century, but serious dangers arise if they are used for more recent periods because they may refer to identifiable people and families. Indeed, most record offices restrict access to log books more than about 50 years old.

13 Other sources

When we were preparing this book, a list of over 200 possible sources was suggested to us! In practice availability, complexity and legibility rule out most of these. This book therefore concentrates on the dozen or so sources which teachers can get hold of and use most easily.

Nevertheless, a number of others, beyond the twelve that have featured in the rest of this book, may be of particular interest to you. The following pages deal briefly with another twelve sources, also arranged alphabetically.

You may be supervising a subject for which some particular local source is ideal. Or perhaps you already know of a local source we do not mention. Naturally, you will need to research and evaluate these individually – though some of our Activities may suggest others possible with your special source.

Apprentice records

Indentures (so called because the document was cut in a wavy line, one half being held by the apprentice, the other by the master) covered the terms of agreement by which a master taught a girl or boy their trade. A stamp duty imposed between 1710 and 1811 results in records being kept which show the apprentice's name and address, the master's name and trade, and (until 1750) the father's name. The Society of Genealogists holds a large collection of these records.

Churchwardens' accounts

In addition to their responsibility for the fabric of the parish church, churchwardens accumulated a great variety of other duties, some of which are illustrated through the accounts they presented to the annual vestry meeting. These commonly include payments for destruction of "vermin" – anything from rats to hedgehogs and sparrows – the storage of the parish armoury of weapons, and especially expenses connected with the enforcement of the harsh anti-vagrancy laws of the 17th century and later. This involved examining paupers and removing them to their parish of settlement, granting settlement certificates, punishing unlicensed beggars and attempting to discover the fathers of illegitimate babies so that the parish did not have to take on their maintenance. Churchwardens' accounts will usually be found in the county record office. They are especially useful for studying the working of the Poor Law, but the handwriting may be difficult to read.

Court rolls

These are descriptions of the cases tried and judgements given in the manor courts of medieval England. They are surprisingly human and interesting documents, throwing light on the very different attitudes of people in medieval times, but can only be considered for school use if local examples have been translated and published in a convenient form.

Domesday Book

William I's great survey of his kingdom was compiled in 1087. A large part of England was covered (but not all parishes), and this is usually the earliest written record to be found. Domesday Book was a record of taxable land; some land was exempt, so is not listed. Not all entries give the same details. It mentions, besides the area of land concerned, such items as the number of plough teams the land would support, the amount of pasture and pannage available, the presence of mills, etc. The original still exists in the Public Record Office in London, but all counties have published translations of local sections, which you should find in your local library. There are also books explaining the terminology, etc.

Film and video

Apart from the National Film Archive, local repositories such as museums, libraries and record offices sometimes hold interesting local material on cine film ranging from amateur footage of war-time activity to training and advertising films made for local firms. Access to this for children may be a problem unless it has been transferred onto video, but it is worth asking what is held locally.

Memorial inscriptions

Gravestones are a source of many useful facts about reasonably well-off people in the past (names, dates, travel, trades and often much else besides). These are usefully studied alongside parish registers. Many are now difficult to read, but CROs, local libraries and the Society of Genealogists hold large collections of transcriptions, some of which relate to memorial inscriptions which today are completely illegible.

Overseers' accounts

Overseers of the poor were appointed in each parish in the 16th century with power to levy a rate on the inhabitants for the relief of those poor born in, or obtaining a settlement in, the parish. Their account books give details of payments made for "out relief", as well as the expenses of the workhouse (before 1834) and some-times of schemes for providing work for the unemployed. See also Churchwardens' accounts.

Poll books

These are lists of property owners between 1696 and 1868 who were eligible to vote. These street by street registers (like modern electoral rolls), are held by CROs and local libraries. Large collections are held by the Institute of Historic Research (University of London), the British Library, the Guildhall Library, London and the Bodleian Library, Oxford.

Quarter Sessions records

These are the records of the county courts which had a wide variety of administrative as well as judicial functions before the establishment of county councils in 1889. Huge collections of papers exist in county record offices, covering everything from the county gaol and transportation of criminals to the maintenance of bridges and the licensing of alehouses and even gamekeepers.

Town records

These are the equivalent of county quarter sessions records in that they cover a wide variety of matters concerning the administration of towns. They may include medieval charters which gave the community independent rights, records of courts, minutes of the common council and later committees such as those for "paving, lighting and watching" the streets after 1836, and many other items. They may be in the town's own record office if it has one, or in the county record office.

Turnpike Trust records

County record offices frequently hold copies of the acts authorising the setting up of turnpike trusts for particular local roads, together with plans of improvements to the route and sometimes the trusts' minutes and accounts. Notices of meetings and of the auctioning of the proceeds of tollgates with the projected income appear regularly in local newspapers.

Workhouse records

Minute books of the Guardians of the Union Workhouse, together with accounts, plans and other materials (not often as lurid and detailed as one might imagine), sometimes survive in county record offices.

Further reading

Listed here are a small number of titles which we feel will be most accessible and helpful to teachers who want to take these topic further. This is only a selection from the many which can be found on most library shelves.

General

Historical Association: *Short Guides to Records, Numbers 1–24, First Series*. Ed. L.M. Munby. Introduction revised by K.L. Thompson and G.C.F. Forster. Reprinted 1994

Historical Association: *Short Guides to Records, Numbers 25–48, Second Series*. Ed. K.L. Thompson. 1993 onwards

Hoskins, W.G.: *Local History in England* (3rd edn. 1984, Longman)

Hoskins, W.G.: *The Making of the English Landscape* (2nd edn. 1992, Hodder & Stoughton; 1991 Penguin)

Richardson, J.: *The Local Historian's Encyclopaedia* (2nd edn. 1986, Historical Publications)

Stephens, W.B.: *Sources for English Local History* (1981, Cambridge University Press)

Tate, W.E.: *The Parish Chest* (2nd edn. 1991, Phillimore)

West, J.: *Town Records* (1983, Phillimore)

West, J.: *Village Records* (1982, Phillimore)

Artefacts

Durbin G., Morris S. and Wilkinson S.: *A Teacher's Guide to Learning from Objects* (1990, English Heritage)

The Centre for Multicultural Education: *Evaluating Artefacts* (1990, Centre for Multicultural Education, Harrison Rd, Leicester LE4 6RB)

Buildings

Brunskill, R.W.: *Traditional Buildings of England: An Introduction to Vernacular Architecture* (1992, Gollancz)

Pevsner, N.: *Buildings of England* (Penguin). County by county; various dates.

Census returns

Public Record Office: *Making Sense of the Census* (1989, HMSO)

Hurley, B. (Ed): *The Book of Trades or Library of Useful Arts (1811) Parts 1 and 2* (Reprinted 1991, 1992 by Wiltshire Family History Society, 21 Elizabeth Drive, Devizes, Wilts SN10 3SB).

Low cost reprints of these contemporary descriptions of how 68 different trades were carried on.

Directories

Shaw, G. and Tipper, A.: *British Directories: A bibliography and guide to directories published in England and Wales (1850-1950) and Scotland (1773-1950)* (1988, Leicester University Press)

Information technology

National Council for Educational Technology: Regular resources and information for teachers. One that is particularly helpful is *Making Links* (ISBN 1 85379 196 2), which outlines several ways IT can help history teachers at KS2. (National Council for Education Technology, Sir William Lyons Rd, University of Warwick Science Park, Coventry CV4 7EZ)

HMI : *Aspects of Primary Education: The teaching and learning of Information Technology* (ISBN 0 11 270770 X, HMSO). Reports and comments on recent trends in IT at primary level

Inventories

Munby, L.: *Reading Tudor and Stuart Handwriting* (1988, British Association for Local History)

West, J.: *Village Records* (1982, Phillimore)

Yarwood, D.: *The English Home* (1956, Batsford)

Maps and air photographs

Harley, J.B.: *Maps for the Local Historian* (1972, Standing Conference for Local History)

Hindle, B.P.: *Maps for Local History* (1988, Batsford)

Ordnance Survey:

Historical maps –   Roman and Anglian York

Viking and Medieval York

Roman and Medieval Bath; and Canterbury

Georgian Bath

Hadrian's Wall

Roman London

Ancient Britain

Roman Britain

Other maps –   Bodleian Map of Great Britain

One inch map of Southampton area, 1810

Oral history

Hewitt, M. and Harris, A.: *Talking time: A guide to oral history for schools* (1992, The Learning Resources Service, Tower Hamlets Education, English St., London E3 4TA. Cost is £8.00, including postage and packing (ISBN 1 873928 89 0))

Perks, R.: *Oral History: An annotated bibliography* (1990, British Library National Sound Archive). Over 2000 references to printed works based on oral evidence; covers a huge variety of topics and places.

Oral History Society: *Oral History* (Journal). Especially volume 20 number 1 (1992), dealing with oral history and the National Curriculum, which includes a useful resource list.

Parish registers

Gwynne, T.: *Local Population Studies in Schools* (Historical Association Teaching of History series, number 53, 1984). Also refers to the use of census data.

Photographs and pictures

Oliver, G.: *Photographs and Local History* (1989, Batsford)

Index of activities